Computer Programming to Insure Project Accountability in Africa

Computer Programming to Insure Project Accountability in Africa

Abdul Karim Bangura

Authors Choice Press

San Jose New York Lincoln Shanghai

Computer Programming to Insure
Project Accountability in Africa

Authors Choice Press
an imprint of iUniverse.com, Inc.

For information address:
iUniverse.com, Inc.
5220 S 16th, Ste. 200
Lincoln, NE 68512
www.iuniverse.com

ISBN: 0-595-19642-X

Printed in the United States of America

To the Afrikan!

Contents

Acknowledgments

I, and hopefully many readers, owe gratitude to:

American University students, for listening to and providing useful comments on the subject. Asking difficult questions often leads to better answers.

Diana Kelly, Fatmata Aminata Bangura and Isatu Ramatu Bangura, for inspiring my preoccupation.

The various families to which I belong, for offering encouragement and prayers.

Introduction

Development economists have traditionally employed Project Appraisal techniques (cost-benefit analysis, profitability analysis, etc.) as the general rationale for ensuring accountability of development projects (e.g., UNIDO 1972, Little and Tipping 1972, Little and Mirrlees 1974, Deepak 1974, Prest and Turvey 1975, Mishan 1976, Hansen 1978, and Irvin 1978). However, project appraisal does not rest on a set of techniques that can be applied mechanically. It is an approach that must be interpreted analytically. Interpretation becomes necessary because, in reality, investment resources are not allocated in a first-best world of perfect competition with no externalities. Instances of market failure and distortions are especially widespread in the developing economies of Africa. The distortions are commonly in foreign trade prices, factor markets, the non-optimal income distribution, and in the use of non-optimal taxes and subsidies. In correcting for these distortions, the practice of project appraisal is an exercise in the theory of the second-best.

Since conditions in African countries diverge from those of the ideal first-best world, we enter a second-best world—a world in which the African development practitioner must operate. The development economist must be concerned with the existence of monopolies, taxes and subsidies, externalities, and price distortions endemic in African economies. When market prices are not honest prices, reflecting real value, or prices do not exist for public goods, then the market prices will no longer equate and equal the marginal social cost (MSC) and the marginal social value

(MSV) of the commodities. [*Marginal* refers to the effects of a change, given the current situation. For example, the marginal cost is the cost of producing an additional unit of a product, given the producer's current facility and production rate.] To remove these distortions, neutral devices should constitute the best remedial policies. So, what is presented in this book is a series of such devices.

Thus, the objective of this book is to present a systematic treatment of a number of computer programming approaches for ensuring accountability of development projects in African countries. This scheme will be important for at least two reasons. First, results obtained in computer programming can be used by practitioners in development project design. Second, techniques used in computational theory, as they pertain to economic development, will serve not only students in computer science, but those in the social sciences as well.

In light of the preceding discussion, the major question in this book is quite straightforward: What salient aspects of computer programming can be developed to insure accountability of development projects in African countries? Underlying this question is the major thesis for this book: that is, salient aspects of computer programming can be developed to insure accountability of development projects in African countries. The systematic application of discovery procedures well-known in computer programming will uncover those salient aspects that can facilitate the creation of such programs.

Basic Organization of the Rest of the Book

Chapter 1 examines advanced programming theory. Chapter 2 is on object- oriented programming. Chapter 3 is about functional programming. Chapter 4 deals with parallel programming. Chapter 5 discusses concurrent programming. Chapter 6 presents a relational model of data. And Chapter 7 is a call for employing a Public Choice approach, buttressed by computer programming techniques, as an alternative for project accountability to facility economic development in Africa. Together, these seven chapters attempt to create a fusion between the disciplines of Computer Science and Economics.

Significance of the Book

This book is significant for at least one major reason: It suggests a series of computer programming techniques that will help to remove distortions in project accountability in African countries. Its originality consists in the clarity with which aspects about computer programming can be employed in economic development project design.

Chapter 1

Advanced Programming Theory

The usefulness of employing Advanced Programming Theory to guide the writing of computer programs that can insure accountability of development projects in African countries hinges on the fact that, while formal language theory was first developed in the mid-1950s in an attempt to generate theories of natural language acquisition, it was soon realized that this theory (particularly the context-free portion) can be quite relevant to the artificial languages that had originated in Computer Science. As Harrison observes, since those days, the theory of formal languages has been developed extensively, and has several discernible trends, which include applications to the syntactic analysis of programming languages, program schemes, models of biological systems, and relationships with natural languages (1978:vii), all of which, consequently, can be applicable to development issues.

In the last twenty years, logic programming has emerged as one of the most promising new programming paradigms and as a very active research area. According to Levi (1994:v), this disciplinary focus was precipitated by two relevant events of the late seventies: (1) the development of the program language Prolog, which soon emerged as one of the most popular tools for declarative programming, and (2) the realization that a subset of first order logic had a very natural interpretation as a programming language, which served as the precursor to the theory of logic programming.

Indeed, during these twenty years, many works have been produced on the subject of logic programming, Prolog and sundry topics relating to them. A majority of these studies are tutorial guides to Prolog programming in the realm of artificial intelligence applications such as expert systems. They vary widely in their level of sophistication and how they acknowledge and exploit underlying logical principles (see, for instance, Apt 1997, Apt and Turini 1995, Apt et al. 1999, Bergadano and Gunetti 1996, Caneghem and Warren 1986, Ceri et al. 1990, Clark and Tärlund 1982, Conery 1987, Doets 1994, Gabbay et al. 1995, Hoare and Stephenson 1985, Hogger 1990, Lavra and Deroski 1994, Levi 1994, Lloyd 1987, Lobo et al. 1992, Manna 1980, Manna and Maldinger 1985, Manna et al. 1977, Saint-Dizier 1994, Saint-Dizier and Szpakowicz 1990).

Thus, before dealing with the issue of using Advanced Programming Theory in insuring the accountability of development projects in Africa, it makes sense to provide the reader with the following background information on logic programming and the advances that have been made in this area. In the end, a conclusion is drawn.

Essentials of Logic Programming

The uncovering of the mathematical content of logic hinges upon two major avenues. The first is **model theory** which examines the relationships between sentences of logic once they have been interpreted, by association with external domain, such as to assign them truth-values. The elementary model theory encompasses vocabulary such as *true, false, interpretation, satisfaction, model, implication,* and *sematic consequence.* The second is **proof theory** which looks at the relationships between sentences in terms of their structural content. Elementary proof theory employs words such as *axiom, inference rule, theorem, proof, consistency* and *syntactic consequence* (Hogger 1990:1). Both approaches are critical for understanding logic programming, and there are simple but vital connections between them when it comes to classical logic. The most important connection is that the things one desires to be true must coincide with the things s/he can prove. In a similar vein, the answers generated by a program should coincide with those that are computable from that program.

Logic programming, as a first approximation, is a computational formalism which combines two key principles: (1) it employs logic to express knowledge; and (2) it employs inference to manipulate knowledge. In the problem-solving context, the first principle is concerned with representing assumptions and conclusions while the second is concerned with establishing the logical connections between assumptions and conclusions. The general objective in such a context is to infer the desired conclusion from the given assumptions, and to do so in a manner which is computationally viable (Hogger 1990:11).

Concretely, the standard formalism employs a particular subset—*clausal-form logic*—of the classical, first-order predicate logic as the language for representing knowledge, and uses a particular inference system—*resolution*—as the mechanism to manipulate knowledge. Furthermore, the logic programming known as Prolog, to be discussed some more later, adds to the kernel logical system clausal-form logic+resolution

a particular sort of control strategy in the pursuit of efficient implementation; the combination of these features is what is called pure Prolog, which is characterized by the fact that the logical analysis of programs written in it does not account for behavioral considerations (Hogger 1990:11).

Thus, as Doets points out, in propositional logic, there are three categories of symbols: (1) variables, (2) connectives, and (3) parentheses. In first-order logical language, he adds, there are seven categories of symbols, as follows (1994:29-30):

(1)   infinitely many (individual variables),

(2)   symbols for the logical operations; next to the connectives 5, „ ″, 6, ‡we now also have the *universal quantifier*   and the *existential quantifier* ,

(3)   symbols indicating grouping: parentheses, and now also the *comma*,

(4)   much later, the *identity symbol* will be used,

(5)   *relation symbols,*

(6)   *function symbols,*

(7)   *constant symbols* or (*individual*) *constants*.

Doets suggests that categories (1) through (4) are fixed for every first-order language, while categories (5) through (7), the so-called *non-logical* symbols, may vary. He also adds that a first-order language is determined by the choice of categories (5) though (7); and thus, a language will be identified with its set of non-logical symbols (1994:30).

Logic program, therefore, is a point of convergence in the disciplines of logic, mechanical theorem-proving and computing science. In particular, logic contributed symbolic systems which benefitted from the economy of syntax and for which the notions of *deriving* sentences and *interpreting* sentences could be independently articulated yet precisely related. For this, much is owed to Gottlob Frege, whose work led to the standard formulation of first-order logic, and Alfred Tarski, who clarified the long-standing semantic conclusions between "truth" and "proof." For the theory of clausal-form logic, much is owed to Jacques Herbrand. The discovery of resolution—a major feat for the mechanization of clausal-form theorem- proving—is owed to J. Alan Robinson. Harnessing of these developments to the service of computer programming was the pioneering work of many individuals, especially Carls Hewitt, Alain Colemerauer and Robert Kowalski (Hogger 1990:14).

Since logic programming enables one to express knowledge explicitly in a machine-independent manner, making programs more compact, flexible and intelligible, many arguments have been advanced in favor of its use. These arguments have been summarized by Hogger as follows (1990:16-17):

(1) Logic programming can be regarded as the corner-stone of **knowledge based programming**. The expressiveness of logic enables one to formulate (encode) assumptions about the problem domain in a direct, implementation-independent manner. Conversely, one can readily decode such a formulation in order to recover its underlying assumptions. Furthermore, the conclusions computed from the formulation are exactly its logical consequences, and so are directly relatable to the assumptions.

(2) *It favours mathematical accountability*—giving precise and simple mathematical characterizations of the relationships between

> programs and the results computed from them
> Programs and specifications
> Programs and other programs.

(3) *It separates knowledge from use*—one can vary the implementation details without affecting the program's logical competence: in particular one can vary either control strategies or machine architectures without necessarily having also to alter programs or their underlying language.

(4) *It offers a uniform paradigm for software technology*—that is, one formalism serves for constructing and manipulating programs, specifications, databases and associated software tools.

(5) *It can be modified or extended in natural ways* to support special forms of knowledge, such as meta-level or higher-order knowledge, as well as to reconstruct ostensibly non-logical formalisms.

(6) Its main conceptual principles can be taught and understood without reference to computer technology—*it can contribute directly to other, non-computational disciplines* relying upon precise means of expression and reasoning.

(7) *It works!*—that is, viable programming technologies have already been founded upon it.

Indeed, the central thesis from the preceding arguments is that the representation and derivation of knowledge is what computing should be all about. Whether or not all, or even a majority of, programmers accept this thesis is another matter.

Parallel Execution of Logic Programs

According to Conery (1987:35), as soon as a user provides an initial goal statement, the execution of a logic program commences. Through a series of resolutions, the interpreter computes values for variables of the goal. The substitutions used in the derivation provide values for the variables of the initial goal, if the null clause can be derived. Where multiple descendants of a node indicate a choice of clauses for resolving the goal at that node, the execution can be represented as a goal tree.

Conery suggests that the two principal forms of parallelism in logic programs can be explained in terms of speeding up the search of the goal tree. The first, *OR parallelism*, is a parallel search strategy: i.e. when a search process reaches a branch in a tree, it starts parallel processes to search each descendant branch. The second, *AND parallelism*, is akin to parallel construction of a branch—i.e. when the interpreter knows a number of steps must be done to complete a branch, it can start parallel processes to perform those steps. While the name for OR parallelism derives from the fact that, in a nondeterministic program, one is often satisfied with any answer, the name for AND parallelism derives from the fact that all steps must succeed in order for a result to be produced (1987:35).

Another way to explicate the distinction, Conery points out, is in terms of the denotation of a goal statement. An interpreter must produce a set of tuples of terms, where each tuple has a value for each variable of the initial goal. While OR parallelism is a method for parallel construction of the different tuples in the denotation of a nondeterministic goal,

AND parallelism is a parallelism in deriving any one tuple. Thus, Conery observes that, in an OR-parallel interpreter, each element is constructed sequentially, employing the same sequence of operations performed by a sequential interpreter. A deterministic goal statement has only one solution; for deterministic goals, an OR-parallel interpreter is no faster in finder an answer than a sequential interpreter which makes perfect decisions at each choice point. An AND-parallel interpreter, Conery adds, has the potential to speed up deterministic computations, since it executes in parallel the necessary steps for constructing the results. In terms of the structure of a program, he further notes, OR parallelism is that obtained from parallel execution of the different clauses of a procedure; AND parallelism is that obtained from parallel execution of the goals in the body of a clause (1987:35, 37).

A third source of parallelism, according to Conery, is that in low-level operations, such as unification. He points out that systems exploiting parallelism at this level are typically sequential interpreters with respect to the global notion of the computation, often executing exactly the same sequence of derivations as a Prolog interpreter (1987:37).

Conery goes on to suggest three broad categories within which abstract models for OR parallelism can be placed. The first category is "pure" OR parallelism, which consists of a parallel search of the goal tree. This is characterized by the fact that, as a searching process comes to a choice point, it can fork new processes for each alternative. From that point, processes proceed with minimal interaction. When a process cannot unify its first literal with any program clause, it simply stops; if it derives the null clause, it announces the result and then stops. No need exists to send information to another active search process. The second category of OR parallelism hinges upon objects referred to as *OR processes*. In this model, a process is like an object of Actors or Smalltalk. Each process must execute a small piece of the program. In addition to maintaining local state information, a process also communicates with other objects through messages. The third category of OR parallelism is *search parallelism*. This is based on a physical partitioning of the program. In this model, clauses are stored in different nodes of a machine such as a multiprocessor database machine. What is common within the models in this category is that unification is done at the nodes where the clauses are stored, and the derivation of resolvents and overall control decisions are executed by a different process (1987:37).

In terms of models for AND parallelism, Conery suggests that, since this type of parallelism is a parallel solution of more than one goal in a given goal statement, the central problem in implementing it is management of variables occurring in more than one literal of the goal statement. He points out that, in a goal statements such as the following,

$$p(X), q(X),$$

the variable X occurs in both goals. Thus, he suggests that to solve this goals statement, one needs to find a value for X that satisfies both p and q. Most abstract models for AND parallelism handle this problem the same way: i.e. they allow only one of the goals to bind the shared variable, and they postpone solution to the others until the variable has been bound. Conery concludes that the models differ in scheduling of goals, the rules for binding shared variables, and whether the goals that bind variables can be nondeterministic (1987:48).

In sum, the parallel execution of logic programs hinges upon the principles of accuracy, modularity, and scalability. The technique can be perceived as an Actors system, requiring many objects to communicate through messages and update local state information in asynchronous operations. It is not surprising, therefore, that local states of objects replace the centralized binding environment usually created in the execution of Prolog programs, and the asynchronous operation of the objects replace the sequential steps of Prolog interpreters. This is quite evident in the following discussion.

From Logic Programming to Prolog

As Apt recounts, the simplicity of the logic programming paradigm caught the attention of researchers interested in theoretical foundations. This is because, by applying methods and techniques of mathematical logic, these researchers could build a rigorous mathematical framework for logic programming. In many instances, these methods must be fine-tuned and appropriately modified to be utilized in logic programming. However, many challenges have been encountered by those who are inclined in more practical aspects of computer science. Consequently, efficient implementation of Prolog and its extensions, development of appropriate programming methodology and techniques, aimed at understanding the logic programming paradigm and, finally, designing various successors and/or improvements of Prolog became an exciting and highly sophisticated field requiring new solutions and fresh insights (1997:1).

According to Apt, when programming in pure Prolog, one needs to adhere to the usual syntactic conventions of the technique. Thus, each query and clause must end with the period "." and in the unit clauses "" is omitted. Unit clauses are referred to as *facts* and non-unit clauses are referred to as *rules*. Indeed, clauses and queries can be broken over several lines. By a *definition* of a relation symbol *p* in a given program *P* means the set of all clauses of *P* which use *p* in their heads. In Prolog, *relation symbol* is a synonym of *predicate*. Strings which begin with a lower-case letter are reserved for the names of function or relation symbols. For instance, f represents a constant, function or relation symbol. Also, each string which begins with a capital letter or "_" (underscore) is identified with a variable. For example Xs is a variable. One begins comment lines with the "%" symbol (1997:105).

However, as Apt suggests, there are two important differences between the syntax of logic programming and of Prolog. The first difference has to do with ambivalent syntax. In first-order logic and, thus, in logic programming, it is assumed that function and relation symbols of different arity make up mutually disjoint classes of symbols. While not explicitly stated, this assumption is a mantra in mathematical logic which can be easily tested by exposing a logician to Prolog syntax and await her/his protests. Namely, unlike first-order logic, in Prolog the *same* name can be utilized for function or relation symbols of different arity. In addition, the same name with the same arity can be employed for function and relation symbols. This facility is what is dubbed *ambivalent syntax* (1997:105).

Apt provides the example that a function or a relation symbol f of arity n is referred to as f/n. So in a Prolog program, one can use both a relation program p/2 and function symbols p/1 and p/2 and build syntactically legal facts such as p(p(a,b), [c,p(a)]). In the presence of ambivalent syntax, the distinction between function symbols and relation symbols and, therefore, between terms and atoms, becomes obsolete. But in the context of queries and clauses, it is clear which symbol refers to which syntactic category. This ambivalent syntax makes it possible for one to employ the same name for naturally related function and relation symbols (1997:105).

The second difference between the syntax of logic programming and of Prolog, according to Apt, hinges upon anonymous variables. Prolog makes it possible to employ anonymous variables written as "_" (underscore). Since each occurrence of "_" in a query or clause is interpreted as a different *variable*, these anonymous variables have a special interpretation. Thus, in definition, each anonymous variable must occur in a query or a clause only once. Apt also mentions that modern versions of Prolog, such as SICStus Prolog, encourage the use of anonymous variables by issuing a warning when a non-anonymous variable that occurs only once in a program is encountered (1997:106).

To compute in Prolog, the leftmost selection rule is first used. This rule allows one to select different atoms in resolvents that happen to occur more than once in the SLD-derivation (computations used to compute answers to a query): i.e. in identical resolvents with different "histories." After that, the clauses are tried in the order in which they appear in the program text. So the program is seen as a *sequence* and not as a set of clauses. Moreover, for the sake of efficiency, the occur-check is omitted from the unification algorithm (Apt 1997:44, 46, 106).

Evident in the preceding discussion is the fact that Prolog combines three aspects of logic programming: i.e. theory, programming, and application. This versatility of Prolog makes it an attractive technique for developing computer programs to insure accountability of development projects in African countries.

Meta-Logics and Logic Programming

Apt and Turini define *meta-programming* as the ability of writing programs that have other programs as data. They point that it is usual to call the programs that play the role of data as *objects programs*, and to the manipulating programs as *meta-programs*. More precisely, they add, meta- programs work on a *representation* of object programs (1995:ix).

According to Apt and Turini, meta-programming has played a primary role both in the foundations of computer science and in its practical developments. The roots of this technique can be traced back to mathematical logic, more specifically to Kleene's normal form theorem that states that for some primitive recursive functions T, U every partial recursive function equals $U(\mu y. T(e,x,y))$ (usually denoted by e) for some natural number e. e can be viewed as the function computed by the program e, and U and T as meta-programs that work on the object program e (1995:ix).

The choice of logic programming as a basis for meta-programming, Apt and Turini suggest, offers certain practical and theoretical advantages. The possibility of tackling critical foundational problems of meta-programming within a framework with a strong theoretical basis is one such advantage. The surprising ease of programming is another advantage. However, as Apt and Turini also note, to formally deal with meta-programs, the usual paradigm of logic programming, or more generally, of first-order logic, has to be modified. This is because, according to them, various phenomena that are relevant to meta-programming, such as the representation of object programs and their syntax, the interplay between the object-level and meta- level, the employment of modules, the representation of proof strategies, and so on, call for logics that are richer and more expressive (1995:ix).

Following Apt and Turini, a classical problem in the foundations of meta-logic programming is the justification of the formally incorrect (untyped) Vanilla meta-interpreter, which employs a non-ground representation of object variables. They suggest that the unwell-typedness of Vanilla leads to the presence of unrelated atoms in the least Herbrand model of the Vanilla meta-interpreter. Therefore, Apt and Turini also argue that, while logic programming is formally based on first-order predicate logic, many of its applications utilize non-standard syntaxes, which are characterized by syntactical ambivalence between formulae, terms, predicates, and functions. They suggest the following as examples: the meta-variable facility of Prolog, the overloading of predicate and functional symbols allowed in Prolog, the identity naming of object-level constructs used in Vanilla meta-programming, and the use of generic predicates in databases (1995:x-xi).

Apt and Turini point out that high-level languages such as Lisp and Prolog are often used for writing meta-programs because the syntactic similarity between programs and data makes it very convenient. If one wants a truly declarative programming language, however, then s/he will be lost in terms of the approach these languages take to meta-programming, because they do not offer the means for a declarative treatment of object variables in the meta-program. Apt and Turini warn that, without a ground representation, only the simplest of meta-programs can have declarative semantics. The caveat, they note, is that employing ground representation apparently incurs a significant overhead in program complexity and computation time. Gödel (to be discussed later), Apt and Turini add, is a new program aimed at narrowing the gap between theory and practice in logic programming, placing particular emphasis on declarative meta- programming. To make this objective a reality, they suggest that Gödel must make the ground representation attractive to programmers in both ease of use and execution time (1995:xii).

Finally, Apt and Turini mention that traditional logic is concerned with static theories, which do not change over the course of time. They also suggest that deductive databases and knowledge bases extend this static form of logic to include the dynamics of database updates and knowledge assimilation. However, they argue that such dynamic theories are still essentially passive in the sense that, although they change their own internal state, they do not change the state of the environment. Meta-logic programming within a concurrent logic programming framework can be employed to extend such theories to active theories, which behave as intelligent agents (1995:xiii).

Indeed, the preceding discussion demonstrates that meta-programming is a powerful technique for extending and modifying the semantics of an existing object language. However, this expressiveness makes meta- programming prone to subtle semantics problems such as the representation of object programs at the meta-level. Nonetheless, through the representation of object-level variables by meta-level variables, one can use meta-logic to create separate object-level programs in various ways to build straightforward and concise meta-programs.

Inductive Logic Programming

Inductive logic programming (ILP) is generally defined as a research area at the intersection of machine learning and logic programming. It is also generally agreed that it aims at a formal framework and practical algorithms for inductively learning logic programs from examples (see, for example, Bergadano and Gunetti 1996:1, Lavra and Deroski 1994:3).

According to Lavra and Deroski, the current interest in machine learning, a subfield of artificial intelligence (AI), hinges upon two reasons. The first reason is that, although there is no consensus on the nature of intelligence, it is nevertheless agreed that the capability of learning is vital for any intelligent behavior. Therefore, machine learning is justified from the scientific perspective as part of cognitive science. The second reason is that machine learning techniques can be successfully employed in knowledge acquisition tools, which is a justification from the engineering perspective. It is essentially accepted that the main barrier in building expert systems, to which the success of AI in industry is largely due, is the acquisition of acknowledge (1994:3).

As part of computer science/engineering, Lavra and Deroski suggest, the goal of machine learning is to create methods, techniques and tools for building intelligent learning systems—for example, such learning programs must be able to change themselves in order to "perform better" at a given task. By "performing better," they mean, for example, to perform more efficiently and/or more accurately. They further note that "better" can also denote the learner's ability to address a broader class of problems (1994:3- 4).

Lavra and Deroski state that, in a broad sense, machine learning paradigms include inductive learning, analytic or deductive learning, learning with genetic algorithms, and connectionist learning—i.e. learning with neural nets. Furthermore, they maintain, several learning paradigms can be integrated within a single multistrategy learning system. And that in a narrower sense, Michie's strong criterion defines learning as an ability to acquire new knowledge by requiring the result of learning to be understandable by humans. In this sense, they argue, connectionist systems are not considered to be learning systems (1994:4).

As Lavra and Deroski also note, induction is generally understood to mean reasoning from specific to general. Thus, according to them, in the case of inductive learning from example, one is given certain examples from which general rules or a theory underlying the examples can be delineated. This is why they also point out that inductive learning has been successfully applied to a variety of classification and prediction problems, such as the diagnosis of a patient or a plant disease, or the prediction of mechanical properties of steel on the basis of its chemical characteristics. These problems, they further suggest, can be formulated as tasks of learning concepts from examples, referred to as *inductive concept learning*, where classification rules for a specific concept must be induced from instances and non-instances of that concept. Thus, to define the problem of inductive concept learning, one must first define a particular concept (1994:4).

In machine learning, one needs to select a formal language for describing objects and concepts. Objects can be described in an object description language, and concepts can be described in the same language or in separate concept description language. In an attribute-value object, description language objects are described by a fixed group of features, also referred to as attributes, each of them taking a value from a corresponding prespecified value set. A concept can also be described extensionally or intensionally. It can be described extensionally by listing the descriptions of all of its instances. It can be described intensionally by using a separate concept description language which allows for more compact and concise concept descriptions, for example, in the form of rules. After selecting description languages for objects and concepts, one needs to develop or use a procedure that will establish whether a given object belongs to a given concept—that is, whether the description of the object satisfies the description of the concept. If it does, then the concept description is said to cover the object description (Lavra and Deroski 1994:4-6).

Thus, Lavra and Deroski, suggest that important performance criteria include the following (1994:9-10):

(1) **Classification accuracy.** The classification accuracy of a hypothesis is measured as the percentage of objects correctly classified by the hypothesis.

(2) **Transparency**. The transparency of a hypothesis denotes the extent to which it is understandable to humans. A possible measure is the *length* of the hypothesis, expressed by the total number of conditions in an induced rule set hypothesis. Another possibility is to measure the number of bits used in the encoding of the description.

(3) **Statistical significance**. Statistical significance tests can be used to evaluate whether a hypothesis represents a genuine regularity in the training examples and not a regularity which is due to chance.

(4) **Information content**. The information content or the relative information score of classifier hypothesis scales the classifier's performance according to the difficulty of the classification problem....

Concept learning can, therefore, be perceived as searching the space of concept descriptions. If one has no background knowledge about the learning problem, s/he learns exclusively from examples. Nonetheless, difficult learning problems typically call for a substantial body of background knowledge. By using this type of knowledge, one may be able to express the generalization of examples in a more natural and concise manner (Lavra and Deroski 1994:10).

In addition, any mechanism used by a learning system to constrain the search for hypotheses is referred to as *bias*. *Declarative bias* is explicit, user-specified bias which can preferably be formulated as a modifiable parameter of the system. Bias can either determine how the hypothesis space is searched (search bias) or determine the hypothesis space itself (language bias). When considering language bias, the expressiveness of a hypothesis language emerges as a critical notion. Expressiveness captures two different dimensions: (1) the expressive power of a formalism—i.e. concepts exist that can be represented in the stronger formalism which cannot be expressed in the weaker formalism; (2) the transparency, or length, of the concept representation (Lavra and Deroski 1994:11:12).

Lavra and Deroski divide ILP systems along four dimensions. The first is learning either a single concept or multiple concepts (predicates). The second is requiring all the training examples to be given before the learning process (batch learners) or accepting examples one by one (incremental learners). The third is, during the learning process, relying on an oracle to verify the validity of generalizations and/or classifying examples generated by the learner. In this case, the learner is referred to as interactive and non-interactive in others. The fourth is trying to learn a concept from scratch or accept an initial hypothesis or theory which is then revised in the learning process. The latter systems are referred to as theory revisors. Although these dimensions are in principle independent, Lavra and Deroski say that existing ILP systems are situated at two ends of the spectrum. At one end are batch non-interactive systems that learn single predicates from scratch; at the other end are interactive and incremental theory revisors that learn multiple predicates (1994:14).

From the preceding discussion, it can be seen that ILP has been concerned with systems and general methods that are given examples and produce programs. Thus, ILS techniques have the potential to support software development and maintenance. This ability is, indeed, critical for developing programs that can insure accountability of development projects in African countries.

From Concurrent Logic Programming to Concurrent Constraint Programming

The popularity of logic programming hinges on the fact that it is an inherently parallel language that is suitable for parallel and distributive architectures. The pure language is already regarded as a model for parallel computation. In what is referred to as process interpretation, the goal is perceived as a system of parallel processes. While the single process evolves through resolution steps, different clausal definitions for the same predicate yield nondeterminism and the shared variables among processes represent communication channels (de Boer and Palamidessi in Levi 1994:55).

Since in a concurrent system processes interact with one another, a concurrent language must embody some synchronization mechanisms and constructs to specify the dependency of choices upon the environment. In addition, the process cannot backtrack once a certain choice has been selected. This principle differs with the kind of nondeterminism of logic programming, according to which all possible solutions are explored—i.e. *the don't know nondeterminism* (Boer and Palamidessi in Levi 1994:55-56).

In concurrent systems, a process cannot "undo" a choice even when it proves to be wrong. This is because a choice and the actions done afterwards have already impacted the environment. To maintain consistency, the entire system should backtrack; however, this approach is extremely inefficient. A preferred solution is to provide the language with mechanisms to control the choices; thus, one should avoid making wrong decisions as much as possible. The most common mechanism for such an approach is the *guard*: that is, a condition associated with each alternative which is tested before selecting that alternative (Boer and Palamidessi in Levi 1994:56).

Almost all concurrent logic languages and concurrent constraints use the *don't care nondeterminism:* that is, clauses are provided with a guard and a process chooses, or commits to, only one clause, as long as its *guard* part is fulfilled. The few languages which maintain don't know nondeterminism, thereby preserving the characteristics of logic programming to compute all solutions, include Distributed Logic, the language of Generalized Horn Clauses, and the language cc(,,). Andorra Prolog combines don't care and don't know nondeterminism (Boer and Palamidessi in Levi 1994:56).

A synchronization mechanism specifies when a process can be activated. In many concurrent programs, synchronization is symbiotic with communication. This is also true for most concurrent logic languages. Earlier concurrent logic languages such as Relational Language, Concurrent Prolog, the language of Guarded Horn Clauses, and Parlog enforced synchronization by introducing a directionality on the communication channels. By so doing, some processes are seen as *producers* (of bindings) on certain variables, while others are seen as *consumers*. The advantage for using such a solution is that the resulting language is write "faithful" to the (parallel) execution model of logic programming: the only necessary modification is with the unification mechanism. This kind of communication is asynchronous in that the process producing a binding and the process consuming (or testing) the binding perform their actions at different times. The opposite of this principle is synchronous communication which requires the partners to exchange the information simultaneously. This latter mechanism has been employed in Distributed Logic, Generalized Horn Clauses, Data Prolog, and the languages of Communicating Clauses (Boer and Palamidessi in Levi 1994:56-57).

P-Prolog is a rather different approach to synchronization that has been proposed. The idea is to suspend process until enough bindings are produced in order for the number of consistent alternatives for the next step reduces to one. This is a semantically clean solution, as it does not modify the declarative reading of the language. Its shortcoming, of course, is that only deterministic processes can be specified in this manner. Such a mechanism is also found in Andorra Prolog and in the ALPS languages (Boer and Palamidessi in Levi 1994:57).

The ALPS paradigm was developed as the concurrent version of Constraint Logic Programming. What it introduced was the *validation* case for the commitment rule. Briefly stated, this rule makes it possible for a process to derive a step using a certain clause only if the constraint established till that moment *entails* the constraint associated with the guard of the clause. This intuition had a strong impact on computer science. A precursor of the ask-rule, it has emerged as one of the central tenets of concurrent constraint programming (CCP) and as the basic synchronization mechanism of concurrent logic/constraint languages (Boer and Palamidessi in Levi 1994:57).

What CCP offers is a novel notion on the underlying philosophy of logic programming. In fact, it is based on extra logical *operators* typical of the concurrent paradigms like CCS, PCSP; particularly, the *choice* (+), the *action prefixing* (), and the *hiding* operator (). Also, concurrent constraint programming entails explicit mechanisms for communication and synchronization consisting of two kinds of actions, *ask* and *tell*. Furthermore, in the concurrent logic languages, these control features, while present, were "hidden" in various ways (Boer and Palamidessi in Levi 1994:57-58).

The explicit representation of these concurrency control mechanisms by means of operators offers many advantages. First, it is the basis for defining a calculus and for an algebraic treatment of processes. Second, the explicit representation allows one to separate each mechanism from the others, thus facilitating a better comprehension of the laws of its behavior. Third, the standard tools developed in the theory of concurrency can be much easily applied. Finally, a "reconciliation" with the declarative principles of logic programming become more feasible. It is not surprising, therefore, that CCP has become rapidly very popular and is regarded as the reference formalism in this area of inquiry (Boer and Palamidessi in Levi 1994:58).

Essentially, CCP can be very useful for developing programs to insure accountability of development projects in African countries because the technique extends logic programming to a language suitable for concurrent systems. Its primary feature is the attempt to define mechanisms for concurrency within the logical paradigm, thereby striving to create a balance between expressiveness and declarative reading.

GÖDEL Programs

Proposed by Hill and Lloyd in 1992, the general-purpose logic programming language (Gödel) places particular emphasis on improving the declarative semantics compared with Prolog. As briefly mentioned earlier, and as Börger and Riccobene also state, Gödel possesses a type of system which is based on many-sorted logic with parametric polymorphism—i.e. a module system and infinite precision integers, rationals, and floating-point numbers. It can solve constraints over finite domains of integers as well as linear rational constraints. It also supports processing of finite sets as well as metalogical facilities, which are created to provide support for meta-programs for analysis, transformation, compilation, verification and debugging of programs (in Levi 1994:231).

In terms of implementation, Börger and Riccobene suggest that nondeterminism reflects the intended flexibility of Gödel's computational rule and the desire "to give implementors the option" of not relying upon some generalization of SLDNF-resolution but of employing "other theorem proving techniques to implement the language, e.g. ones which avoid floundering or are more complete." By stepwise refinement, a mathematically precise, but simple, procedural formalization of the language which describes the full control flow behavior of Gödel programs on the basis of abstract machine and resolution independent search spaces is developed. In particular, the model for an SLDNF-like resolution as a basic computational mechanism can be exemplified in a modular way and exhibit specifically the interface where one can

(a)   adapt the semantics to possible future changes in the design of the language,

(b)   refine it in terms of particular proof systems or lower level specifications which are driven by consideration of execution efficiency and similar implementation issues (in Levi 1994:232).

Gödel's search spaces are similar to those of Prolog tree algebras, which are presented in hybrid stack oriented form as a basis for a formal model of Prolog. The abstract search spaces are obtained from Prolog tree algebras by a further abstraction step, introduced to directly reflect the desired flexible character of Gödel's computational rule. This rule, which is nondeterministic, is as follows (Börger and Riccobene in Levi 1994:232):

(a) in choosing where the next deduction step takes place, thus abstracting in particular from PROLOG's depth-first strategy,

(b) in selecting, out of a conjunction of goals, the literal to be computed, thus abstracting from PROLOG's left-to-right strategy,

(c) in selecting a clause to reduce the current call, thus abstracting from PROLOG's sequential strategy and from any scheme for indexing, switching, last call optimization, etc.

Moreover, Gurevich's concept of *external* functions in *evolving algebras* provides the technical instrument to express in an explicit and transparent manner the role of the three pairwise orthogonal nondeterministic control components for the semantics of Gödel and in general logic programs. The effect of control by delaying, pruning, conditionals, negation, etc. on program execution is represented by abstract conditionals. These can be perceived as directives for the implementation of efficient, but semantically correct, search strategies. This facilitates a highly abstract mathematical paradigm for logic programming systems which will permit one to conduct a comparative study of the different answers which have been provided (Börger and Riccobene in Levi 1994:232-233).

In light of the preceding discussion, the usefulness of the Gödel programming language for the development of a program that will insure accountability of development projects in African countries hinges on the fact that the formalization of the language directly reflects the intuitive procedural understanding of programs. However, it is formulated at the level of abstract search spaces and proceeds in a modular manner. This combination of procedural and abstract features, facilitated by use of Gurevich's idea of evolving algebras, gives one a tool for mathematical (machine and proof system independent) description and analysis of design decisions for logic programming languages. Through a hierarchy of specifications at lower levels, down to implementations, Gödel also lays the ground for provable correct stepwise refinements.

Using Advanced Programming Theory for African Development Projects

There are many reasons Advanced Programming Theory is relevant in writing computer programs to deal with development project accountability. To begin with, formal language theory concerns itself with sets of strings called "languages" and different techniques for generating and recognizing them. Certain finitary processes for generating these sets are referred to as "grammars" (Harrison 1978:1, Howie 1991:40, Moret 1998:44). Phrase-structure grammars are, therefore, fundamental for developing computer programs for development project accountability. Also, Ramsey's Theorem, which is a deep and very general combinatory theorem, is useful for showing relationships that must hold in any sufficiently long word in developing such programs. In addition, a classical theorem of analysis due to Lagrange can be applied to power series generated by context-free grammars and can be employed to solve for the "degree of ambiguity" that is endemic in such programs (Harrison 1978:1- 2).

Regular project development events, or the sets accepted by finite automata, can be characterized by a class of context-free grammars as well. This fulfills one of the requirements of the Chomsky Hierarchy—phrase-structure, type-o, context-sensitive with erasing; context-sensitive with monotonic; context-free; *LR(k)*; linear; right linear, left linear (Harrison 1978:20, 45, Howie 1991:188).

It is also possible to eliminate variables that can never occur in sentential form as well as variables that can never generate a terminal string. Substituting context-free languages into context-free languages gives context-free languages—a characterization of regular sets that involves self-embedding grammars (Harrison 1978:73, Howie 1991:95).

There exist many different types of context-free grammars that can generate all of the context-free languages. Such results are of general interest because, if one wishes to show that some set is context-free, it is easier if one can use the full generality of context-free grammars so that s/he can exploit -rules, chain rules, left incursion, etc. However, if one wishes to show that some property does *not* hold, it will be convenient for her/him to restrict the type of grammar severely, since the complexity of a proof can be reduced (Harrison 1978:93). Thus, a number of normal forms used here can be useful in practical applications to parsing in programs developed for development project accountability.

Pushdown automata (i.e. automata consisting of three parts: read-only input tape, a read-write Pushdown store, and a finite state control) can be an important and satisfying theorem in greatly strengthening one's intuition about which sets are context-free. In addition, *Deterministic* context-free languages are all unambiguous and, moreover, are recognizable in real time. This family of languages are, therefore, very practical for compiler writers and those interested in fast parsing techniques (Harrison 1978:135, Howie 1991:122). This is decidedly necessary for development project design.

An iteration theorem for context-free languages permits one to give direct proofs that certain sets are not context-free. This theorem also demonstrates that, over one-letter terminal alphabet, there is no difference between context-free and regular sets. Consequently, an important result is that context-free languages are closed under "sequential transducer mappings" (Harrison 1978:185).

A language can be inherently ambiguous if every one of its infinitely many context-free grammars was ambiguous. Thus, there are inherently ambiguous languages that have an exponential number of derivation trees in the length of the string. And since the number of factorizations of a string of length n is exponential in n, this is as many as can be (Harrison 1978:233).

Context-free grammars and languages from the point of view of actually computing certain information aid in answering the question whether there exist algorithms to determine, say, $L(G) = \emptyset$ or $L(G_1) = {}^*$. The halting problem for Turing machines can be reviewed formally, and the Post correspondence problem can be defined and shown to be unsolvable by reduction to the halting problem. One can also consider problems like "given a context-free language *(LG)*, can one decide whether *(LG)* is deterministic." Of course, that problem is unsolvable. By replacing "deterministic" by, say, "finitely inherently ambiguous," then the answer is the same (Harrison 1978:247, Howie 1991:43, Morel 1998:100).

Context-sensitive languages and phrase-structure languages can be characterized in terms of Turing machines. For the former, one needs to restrict attention to nondeterministic, linearly space-bounded devices. This pays attention on both time- and space-bounded computations of nondeterministic and deterministic Turing machines. For instance, all context-sensitive languages are recursive, but there exist recursive sets that are not context-sensitive (Harrison 1978:271).

In order that languages that are generated are exactly context-free languages, various restrictions can be placed on phrase-structure grammars or on their derivations. Also, the semi-Dyck and Dyck sets are sets with several types of left and right brackets that can be balanced according to one-sided or two-sided cancellation rules (Harrison 1978:299, Howie 1991:32, 95, 115, 117).

It also is possible to construct efficient parsers for deterministic context- free languages, which are the most important classes of languages. One then gains a certain advantage by employing the more tractable subfamily of strict deterministic languages. Consequently, a language is strict deterministic if and only if it is both deterministic and prefix-free. This enables one to prove iteration theorems for both strict deterministic and deterministic languages. For example, the family of simple languages—i.e. those accepted by one-state real-time dpda's which accept by empty store— has an unsolvable problem but a solvable equivalence problem (Harrison 1978:333-4).

Since one of the vital applications of language theory concerns the recognition and parsing of context-free languages, such recognizers become the core of many programs that take their input in natural-language form. Even though some of these systems employ more sophisticated types of grammars, such as transformational grammars, even these hinge on a context-free base. And since there exist a "hardest" context-free language in terms of recognizing time and space, there also exist techniques for doing elementary operations to computing the transitive closure of a matrix—e.g., the Cooke-Kasami-Younger algorithm (Harrison 1978:417, Howie 1991:29, 82, Morel 1998:114, 200, 203).

Finally, the class of *LR(k)* grammars, which have the property that they can be parsed in linear time, is large enough to allow one to accommodate "natural grammars" for programming languages. Of course, all deterministic languages have an *LR(k)* grammar so that the family of languages is nontrivial and has desirable practical properties such as unambiguity. Thus, every strict deterministic language is *LR(O)* and every deterministic language is *LR(1)* (Harrison 1978:501).

Conclusion

The primary goal of this chapter was to provide an account of how Advanced Programming Theory of formal languages can be employed for writing computer programs that can insure accountability for development projects in African countries. Those applications of the subject to syntactic analysis and some material of that subject have been included in the discussion.

It should be noted that one of the difficulties facing anyone using formal language theory is how to present the results. This is because the proofs in language theory are often constructive and the verifications that the constructions work can be long.

Chapter 2

Object-Oriented Programming

"Over the past few years," asserts Booch, "object-oriented (OO) technology has evolved in diverse segments of the computer sciences as a means of managing the complexity inherent in many different kinds of systems. The object model has proven to be a very powerful and unifying concept" (1994:v). It is this characteristic of OO Programming (OOP) that will make it quite suitable for employing it in insuring development project accountability in African countries. Indeed, it is this characteristic that has made it possible for the OO paradigm to be used throughout the world for such diverse domains as the administration of banking transactions, the automation of bowling alleys, the management of public utilities, the mapping of the human genome, and for writing new generation operating systems such as avionics systems, database systems, multimedia applications, telephony systems, etc. Many such projects employ OO technology because there seems to be no other way to economically produce a lasting and resilient programming system (see, for example, Blair 1991, Braude 1998, Burnett et al. 1995, Fayad and Laitinen 1998, Halladay and Wiebel 1993, Joyner 1999, Kung et al. 1998, Lieberherr 1996, Lieberman 1991, Morris 1994, Palsberg and Schwartzbach 1994, Rosenberg and Koch 1990, Tkach and Puttick 1996, and Wilkie 1993).

A major aspect of OOP is that programming in an OO language is more than just learning new functions, syntax, etc. For instance, when a person studies COBOL, another procedural language, s/he could simply apply the knowledge gained from learning Modula-2 to COBOL. This cannot be done with OO languages, because they require a new way of thinking about decomposition. The person is forced to think not in terms of data structures, but in terms of objects—i.e. a bundle of variables and related methods, or, according to Halladay and Wiebel, "abstract data types" (1993:6). In essence, the differences hinge upon the fact that, while structured design methods build upon structured programming, OO design builds upon OO programming.

The undergirding notion of an object is that of simulation. While most programs are written with very little reference to the real world objects with which they are designed to work, in OO methodology a program should be written to simulate the states and activities of real world objects. This calls for a programmer to not only look at data structures when modeling an object, but to also look at methods associated with that object—i.e. functions that modify the objects' attributes. The following example explicates this concept.

Say one wants to write a program about a bag of rice. If the person were writing this program in Modula-2, s/he could write something like this:

```
TYPE RiceType=Record
        RiceName:           STRING:
        PoundsInBag:        REAL;
        Grain:              GrainType
        Variety:            REAL:


BagsNeededForAFamilyOfFiveForOneMonth:
CARDINAL;
                ...
        END;
```

Now if the person wants to initialize a bag of rice, it will be coded in Modula-2 as follows:

```
VAR MyBag:   RiceType;

BEGIN
        ...
        (* Initialize (i.e. buy) a bag: *)
        MyBag.Ricename:="Jasmine";
        MyBag.PoundsInBag:=25;
        ...
        ...
        (* Take a bag *)
        MyBag.PoundsInBag := MyBag.PoundsInBag-25;
        ...
```

The person has constructed this entire model based on data types. That is, s/he defined RiceType as a record structure and gave that structure various names, e.g., Name. This is the norm for procedural programming.

This is, however, not how one looks at things when s/he wants to program using objects. S/he would have to deal with methods. This means that when the person takes a real world object, in this case a bag of rice, when s/he wants to model it using computational objects, s/he not only looks at the structure of which it consists, but also all possible operations that s/he might want to perform on that data. For the example here, the person should also define the following methods associated with RiceType object:

o IntializeRice (this should allow the person to give the rice a name, a weight/pounds, etc)

o GetPounds (to see much more rice is left)

o Take_A_Bag (for a family of five for one month)

o Take_A_HalfBag (for a husband and a wife for one month)

o Take_A_QuarterBag (for a single person for one month)

There are many more methods the person can define. For example, s/he may want a function GetRiceName to help her/him order another variety of rice.

Thus, the major reason for OOP's usefulness is that it is built upon a sound engineering foundation, whose elements are collectively refereed to as the *object model*—a model that encompasses the principles of abstraction, encapsulation, modularity, hierarchy, typing, concurrency, and persistence. While these principles are not new in the computer sciences, their importance in terms of the object model is that they are brought together in a synergistic manner. The next subsection of this paper outlines these principles. In the subsection that follows, these principles are concretized through the discussion of an OO model for insuring accountability in an inventory tracking system of providing high-yield seeds to farmers in African countries. However, before doing this, it is imperative that clear definitions be provided for the three foundations of the object model: i.e. object-oriented programming (OOP), object-oriented design (OOD), and object-oriented analysis (OOA). The following definitions are from Booch (1994:38-39):

(a) **Object-Oriented Programming** is a method of implementation in which programs are organized as cooperative collections of objects, each of which represents an instance of some class, and whose classes are all members of a hierarchy of classes united via inheritance relationships.

(b) **Design** is a method of design encompassing the process of object-oriented decomposition and a notation for depicting both logical and physical as well as static and dynamic models of the system under design.

(c) **Object-Oriented Analysis** is a method of analysis that examines requirements from the perspective of the classes and objects found in the vocabulary of the problem domain.

The relationship between these three foundations of OOP hinges upon the fact that the products of OOA serve as the models from which an individual may start an OOD; the products of OOD can then be employed as guideposts for the complete implementation of a system using OOP methods.

Principles of the Object Model

As mentioned earlier the principles of the object model include abstraction, encapsulation, modularity, hierarchy, typing, concurrency, and persistence. These principles are outlined in this subsection.

Abstraction "denotes the essential characteristics of an object that distinguish it from all other kinds of objects and thus provide crisply defined boundaries, relative to the perspective of the viewer" (Booch 1994:41). In essence, abstraction is one of the fundamental ways that will allow a programmer to deal with the complexity inherent in insuring accountability in development projects. This is because a good abstraction emphasizes details that are significant to the reader and user and suppresses those that are immaterial or diversionary (for details, see, for example, Halladay and Wiebel 1993:31-32, Burnett et al. 1995:211-225, and Fayad and Laitinen 1998:31-34).

Encapsulation refers to "the process of compartmentalizing the elements of an abstraction that constitute its structure and behavior; encapsulation serves to separate the contractual interface of an abstraction and its implementation" (Booch 1994:50). Indeed, encapsulation is complimentary to abstraction, since the latter focuses upon the observable behavior of an object while the former focuses upon the implementation that gives rise to the behavior in the first place (for details, see, for example, Cohen and Booch 1996:22, Rosenberg and Koch 1989:141, Tkach and Puttick 1996:22, and Joyner 1999:21-25). Encapsulation then becomes critical for insuring accountability in development projects because it is most often achieved through information hiding—i.e. the process of hiding all secrets of an object that do not contribute to its essential characteristics.

Modularity is that "property of a system that has been decomposed into a set of cohesive and loosely coupled modules" (Booch 1994:57). Modularity allows a programmer to divide a program into individual components in order to reduce its complexity to a certain degree (for more on this, see Lieberherr 1996:24 & 30, and Blair et al. 1991:39). Especially for larger applications, such that exist for development projects, and in which many hundreds of classes exist, the use of modules is essential for managing complexity.

Hierarchy refers to "a ranking or ordering of abstractions" (Booch 1994:59). There are two types of hierarchy: (1) *single inheritance* in which one class shares the defined structure or behavior defined in one class, and (2) *multiple inheritance* in which one class shares the structure or behavior defined in two or more classes (Booch 1994:59). As a set of abstractions often forms a hierarchy, identifying these hierarchies in a design helps a programmer to simplify her/his understanding of the problem (refer to Morris 1994:23, Wilkie 1993:27, and Lieberman 1991:8). Thus, hierarchy becomes critical for designing a program that would insure accountability of development projects in Africa because inheritance denotes an "is-a" relationship, which implies a generalization/specialization hierarchy in which a subclass specializes the more general structure or behavior of its superclass.

Typing "is the enforcement of the class of an object, such that objects of different types may not be interchanged, or at the most, they may be interchanged only in very restricted ways" (Booch 1994:66). The concept of a *type*, which derives primarily from the theories of abstract data types, allows for the characterization of structural and behavioral properties that are shared by a collection of entities (for details, consult, for example, Palsberg and Schwartzbach 1994:3-48 passim, Burnett 1995:142-179 passim, and Wilkie 1993:31, 174, 194, 204, 212 & 219). Typing, therefore, will assist an individual to design a program that would insure accountability of development projects in African countries because s/he will be able to express abstractions so that the programming language in which they will be implemented can be made to enforce design decisions.

Concurrency is that "property that distinguishes an active object from one that is not active" (Booch 1994:74). Since for certain kinds of problems an autonomous system may have to handle many different events as the same time, and for other kinds so much computation may be required that exceed the capacity of a single processor, it makes sense to consider using a distributed set of computers for the target implementation or to use processors capable of multitasking (for details, see, for instance Blair et al. 1991:304, Rosenberg and Koch 1990:11-14, Joyner 1999:253-266,

Halladay and Wiebel 1993:194, and Fayad and Laitinen 1998:75-76). The essence of concurrency then for creating a program to insure accountability of development projects in African countries hinges upon its ability to focus on process abstraction and synchronization. As such, development projects can be conceptualized as phenomena existing in a world consisting of a set of cooperative objects, some of which are active and, thus, serve as centers of independent activity.

Persistence refers to "the property of an object through which its existence transcends time (i.e. the object continues to exist after its creator ceases to exist) and/or space (i.e. the object's location moves from the address space in which it was created" (Booch 1994:77). Thus, persistence encompasses many attributes: (a) transient results in expression evaluation; (b) local variables in procedure activations; (c) own variables, global variables, and heap items whose extent is different from their scope; (d) data that exist between executions of a program; (e) data that exist between various versions of a program; (f) data that outlive the program (e.g., Booch 1994:75-77, Blair et al. 1991:190-192, and Rosenberg and Koch 1990:10- 11). For an individual developing a program to insure accountability of development projects in African countries, persistence is critical because s/he must think of objects that can move from machine to machine, and that may even be represented differently on different machines.

Thus, from the preceding discussion, applying the object model in a program that will help to insure accountability in a development project in Africa will be fundamentally different from traditional methods of structured analysis, structured design, and structured programming. This is not to suggest that the object model abandons all of the sound principles and experiences of these older models. Rather, several novel elements must be introduced to build upon these models. In that respect, the object model offers a number of substantive benefits that other models simply cannot make available. Thus, the object model can allow a person to design a project accountability program that will embody the following five attributes of a well-structured complex systems that have been suggested by some computer programmers: (1) exploitation of the expressive power of object-based and object-oriented programming languages; (2) reuse not only of software but of entire designs, leading to the creation of reusable application frameworks; (3) production of systems that are built upon stable intermediate forms, which are more resilient to change; (4) reduction of risks inherent in developing complex systems, since integration is spread out across the life cycle rather occurring as one major event; (5) appealing to the workings of human cognition. All of these attributes are evident in the following example.

An Inventory Tracking System for Supplying High-Yield Seeds to African Farmers

Indeed, it is no exaggeration to assert that the object model has proven applicable to a wide variety of problem domains. As the example in this subsection illustrates, OOA and OOD can be employed to effectively attack the complexity inherent in very large systems such as development projects in African countries.

As Booch observes, for many business applications, companies use off-the-shelf database management systems (DBMS) to provide generic solutions to the problems of persistent data storage, concurrent database access, data integrity, security, and backups. These DBMS are adapted to the given business enterprises, and organizations traditionally approach this task by separating it into two different ones: data design is given to the to database experts, and software design is given to application developers. While this approach has certain advantages, it also does involve some real problems. Due to their different technologies and skills, cultural differences do exist between database designers and programmers. Database designers tend to perceive the world in terms of persistent, monolithic tables of information, whereas application developers tend to perceive the world in terms of its flow of control (1994:377).

In addition, Booch notes, it is impossible to achieve integrity of design in a complex system without reconciling the concerns of these two groups. In a system in which data issues dominate, an individuals is behooved to make intelligent trade-offs between a database and its applications. A database schema designed without taking into consideration its use is both inefficient and clumsy. Likewise, applications developed in isolation place unreasonable demands upon the database and often lead to serious problems of data integrity because of the redundancy of data (1994:377).

Moreover, Booch adds, traditional mainframe computing in the past raised some very real walls around an organization's database assets. However, in the advent of low-cost computing, which places personal productivity tools in the hands of a multitude of workers, coupled with networks that serve to link personal computers across offices as well as across nations, the face information management systems has been irreversibly changed. A major part of this change involves the application of client/server architectures (1994:378). In the following paragraphs, an example of a Management Information System (MIS) application is provided to show how object-oriented technology can address the issue of database and application design in a unified manner, in the context of a government client/server architecture in an African country.

Defining the Boundaries of the Problem. An inventory tracking system of supplying high-yield seeds to African farmers is a highly complex application whose use touches virtually every aspect of the workflow within a development project. The physical warehouse exists to store products, but it is this software that will serve as the warehouse's soul, for without it, the warehouse will not function as an efficient distribution center.

Part of the challenge in developing such a comprehensive system is that it requires planners to rethink their entire operation, yet balance this with the capital investment they already have in other systems. While productivity gains can sometimes be made simply by automating existing manual processes, radical gains are usually only achieved when some of the basic assumptions about how the operation runs are challenged. How this operation is reengineered is a system-planning activity, and so is outside the scope of this paper. However, just as software architecture bounds an implementation problem, so too does the operation's vision bound the entire software problem. One therefore begins by considering an operational plan for running the warehouse. Systems analysis suggests that there are seven major functional activities in such an operation:

(1) Order entry—responsible for taking farmers' orders and for responding to farmers' queries about the status of their orders

(2) Accounting—responsible for sending invoices and tracking farmers' payments (accounts receivable) as well as for paying government suppliers for orders from purchasing (accounts payable)

(3) Shipping—responsible for assembling packages of high-yield seeds for shipment in support of filling farmers' orders

(4) Stocking—responsible for placing new inventory in stock as well as for retrieving inventory in support of filling farmers' orders

(5) Purchasing—responsible for ordering stock from suppliers and tracking supplier shipments

(6) Receiving—responsible for accepting stock from suppliers

(7) Planning—responsible for generating reports to management and studying trends in inventory levels and farmers' activity

Not surprisingly, the required system architecture will be isomorphic to these functional units. The network will actually be quite a common MIS structure: banks of personal computers feed a central database server, which in turn serves as a central repository for all the enterprise's interesting data.

A few details about this network is called for. First, there should be nothing in the software architecture that constrains a specific personal computer (PC) to only a single activity: the accounting department should be able to perform general queries, and the purchasing department should be able to query accounting records concerning supplier payments. This way, as changing operations conditions dictate, management can add or reallocate computing resources as needed to balance the daily workflow. Obviously, security requirements call for some management discipline: for instance, a stock person should not be allowed to send out checks. Constraints for this type of responsibility are necessary for operational consideration, carried out by general network access-control mechanisms that either constrain or grant right to certain data and applications.

As part of this system architecture, it is also assumed that there exists a local area network (LAN) that ties all of the computing resources together, and provides common network services such as electronic mail, shared directory access, printing, and communications. From the perspective of the suggested inventory tracking system software, the choice of a particular LAN is largely immaterial, as long as it provides these services reliably and efficiently.

The availability of hand held PCS as part of the stocking function adds a new wrinkle to this network. The economies of notepad and specialized PCS, carried on a belt together with wireless communications, make it possible to consider an operational plan that takes advantage of these technologies to increase productivity. Basically, the plan will be to give each stock person a hand held PC. As new inventory is placed in the warehouse, they use these devices to report the fact that the stock is now in place, and also notify the system where it is located. As orders of the day are assigned to be filled, packing orders are transmitted to these devices, directing workers where to find certain stock, as well as how many of each to retrieve to pass on to shipping.

Indeed, this technology is not complicated—everything in this network is essentially off-the-shelf hardware. Nonetheless, a bit of new software needs to be developed as well. It makes a great deal of sense to buy rather than to build commercial spreadsheets, GroupWise products, and accounting packages. However, what breathes life to this system is its inventory-tracking software, which ties everything together.

Such an application performs relatively little computational work. Instead, large volumes of data must be stored, retrieved, and moved about. Most of the architectural work will, thus, involve decisions about the declarative knowledge (existing entities, their meanings, and their locations) rather than procedural knowledge (the happening of things). The soul of the design hinges upon the central concerns of object-oriented development: i.e. major abstractions that form the vocabulary of the problem domain and the mechanisms that manipulate them.

Operational demands call for the inventory-tracking system to be, by its very nature, open-ended. During analysis, the major abstractions to the operation at the time will be understood. To be identified are the kind of data that must be stored, the reports to be generated, the procedures of the operation. Over time, new high-yield seeds will be managed by each warehouse, new farmers and suppliers will be added, and old ones removed. Operational use of the system may pinpoint the unanticipated need to capture additional information about the farmer.

Scenarios. Now that the scope of the system has been established, the next thing to do in the analysis is to examine several scenarios of its use. One begins by enumerating a number of primary use cases in terms of the various functional elements of the system as follows:

o   A farmer places an order at the local agricultural office.

o   A farmer checks to find out about the status of the order.

o   A farmer adds items or removes items from an existing order.

o   A stock person receives a packing order to retrieve stock

o   Shipping receives an assembled order and prepares it for shipping.

o   Accounting prepares an invoice.

o   Purchasing places an order for new inventory.

o   Purchasing adds or removes a new supplier.

o   Purchasing queries the status of an existing supplier order.

o   Receiving accepts a shipment from a supplier, placed against a standing purchase order.

o   A stock person places new stock into inventory.

o   Accounting cuts a check against a purchase order for new inventory.

o   The planning department generates a trend report, showing the sales activity for various high-yield seeds.

o   For tax-reporting purposes, the planning department generates a summary report showing current inventory levels.

For each of these primary scenarios, a number of secondary ones can be envisioned as follows:

o   A variety of high-yield seeds a farmer requested is out of stock or on backorder.

o   A farmer's order is incomplete, or mentions incorrect or obsolete product numbers.

o   A farmer queries about or changes an order, but cannot remember what exactly was ordered, by whom, or when.

o   A stock person receives a packing order to retrieve stock, but the item cannot be found.

o   Shipping receives an incompletely assembled order.

o A farmer fails to pay an invoice.

o Purchasing places an order for new inventory, but the supplier has gone out of business or no longer carries the item.

o Receiving accepts an incomplete shipment from a supplier.

o Receiving accepts a shipment from a supplier for which no purchase order can be found.

o A stock person places new stock into inventory, only to discover that there is no space for the item.

o A business tax code changes, requiring the planning department to generate a number of new inventory reports.

By anthropromorphizing for each of the suggested system's functions, many of the interesting high-level objects within the system will be discovered. To begin with, a list of the various people that interact with the system is generated as follows:

o Farmer

o Supplier

o OrderAgent

o Accountant

o ShippingAgent

o StockPerson

o PurchasingAgent

o ReceivingAgent

o Planner

This list also suggests the following key abstractions, each of which stands for some information manipulated by the system:

o FarmerRecord

o ProductRecord

o SupplierRecord

o Order

o PurchaseOrder

o Invoice

o PackingOrder

o StockingOrder

o ShippingLabel

In this case, the classes "FarmerRecord," "ProductRecord," and "SupplierRecord" parallel the abstractions "Farmer" and "Supplier." Both sets of abstractions must be retained, since each plays a subtly different role in the system.

For such a complex system that is suggested here, one would expect to identify dozens of primary scenarios and many more secondary ones. As a matter of fact, several weeks will be needed just to deal with this part of the analysis. In short, the preceding list is incomplete. Nonetheless, sufficient information has been provided to move on to architectural design. Before doing so, however, it is imperative that consideration be given first to some principles that will influence the design decisions about the structure of data within the system.

Database Model. Instead of a hierarchical, a network, or a relational model, an object-oriented database model (OODBMS) will be used for the inventory-tracking system. According to Booch,

> An OODBMS represents a merging of traditional database technology and the object model. OODBMSs have proven to be particularly useful in domains such as computer-aided engineering (CAE) and computer-aided software engineering (CASE) applications, for which we

must manipulate significant amounts of data with a rich semantic content. For certain applications, object-oriented databases can offer significant performance improvements over traditional relational databases. Specifically, in those circumstances where we must perform multiple joins over many distinct tables, object-oriented databases can be much faster than comparable relational databases. Furthermore, object-oriented databases provide a coherent, nearly seamless model for integrating data with business rules. To achieve much the same semantics, RDBMS [relational database management systems] usually require complex triggering functions, generated through a combination of third- and fourth-generation languages— not a very clean model at all (1994:292).

Considering a database of high-yield seeds for a version of the inventory-tracking system suggested here, the products must be uniquely identified by a product identification number, along with a descriptive part name. Products come from suppliers; so for each supplier, a unique identification number, a company name, an address, and perhaps a telephone number must be maintained. Moreover, the inventory must be tracked via a table containing the quantity of all products that are on hand. In the presence of an object-oriented schema, this implementation secret is hidden from all application clients. Thus, it becomes the responsibility of the "ProductRecord" class to provide the illusion of *quantity* as being an integral part of the abstraction.

Structured Query Language (SQL). Given the object-oriented view of the world of development projects, wherein the data and behavioral aspects of the preceding abstractions are united, a user might want to perform a variety of common transactions upon generated tables. For example, s/he might want to add new high-yield seeds suppliers, delete products, or update quantities in the inventory. The person might also want to query these tables in a variety of ways. For instance, s/he might want a report that lists all the high-yield seeds s/he can order from a particular supplier. The person might also want a report listing the high-yield seeds whose inventory is either too low or too high, according to some criteria s/he gives it. Finally, the person might want a comprehensive report giving her/him the cost to restock the inventory to certain levels, using the inexpensive sources of high-yield seeds. These kinds of transactions being common in almost every application of an RDBMS led to the emergence of a standard language called Structured Query Language (SQL) for interacting with relational databases. SQL is employed either interactively or programmatically.

The most important construct in SQL is the select clause, which is represented as follows (Booch 1994:396):

```
SELECT      <attribute>
FROM        <relation>
WHERE       <condition>
```

For example, to retrieve high-yield seeds product numbers for which inventory is less than 500, one might write:

```
SELECT      PRODUCTID, QUANTITY
FROM        INVENTORY
WHERE       QUANTITY<500
```

Much more complicated selection can be made. For example, one might want the same report to include the part name of a variety of high-yield seeds instead of its part number:

```
SELECT      NAME, QUANTITY
FROM        INVENTORY, PRODUCTS
WHERE       QUANTITY<500
AND         INVENTORY.PRODUCT=
            PRODUCTS.PRODUCTID
```

The preceding clause represents a *join*—i.e. the combination of two or more relations into a single relation. The preceding select clause does not generate a new table; instead, it returns a set of rows. Since a single selection might return some arbitrarily large number of rows, one must have some means of going to each at a time. The cursor is used in SQL for that purpose. For example, a user might declare a cursor as follows:

```
DECLARE C CURSOR
        FOR SELECT NAME, QUANTITY
            FROM INVENTORY, PRODUCTS
            WHERE       QUANTITY < 500
            AND         INVENTORY.PRODUCTID =
                        PRODUCTS.PRODUCTID
```

To cause evaluation of this join, the person can write:

```
OPEN C
```

Then to visit each row from the join, s/he writes:

```
FETCH C INTO NAME, AMOUNT
```

Finally, when the person is done, s/he closes the cursor by executing:

```
CLOSE C
```

Instead of employing a cursor, one may generate a virtual table that entails the result of the selection. Such a virtual table is referred to as a *view*, which is just as operational as an actual table. For example, to create a view containing the part name, high-yield seeds supplier name, and cost, one might write:

```
CREATE VIEW V (NAME, COMPANY, COST)
        AS SELECT   PRODUCTS.NAME,
                    SUPPLIERS.COMPANY, PRICES.PRICE
        FROM        PRODUCTS, SUPPLIERS, PRICES
        WHERE       PRODUCTS.PRODUCTID=
                    PRICES.PRODUCTID
        AND         SUPPLIERS.SUPPLIERID=
                    PRICES.SUPPLIERID
```

Thus, according to Booch (1994:397), views are particularly important because they allow different users to have different views upon the database. Since views may be quite different from the underlying relations in the database, they can allow for a degree of data independence. Writing of secure transactions is also possible, because access rights may also be granted to users on a view-by-view basis. Views are a little different from base tables, however, in that the former representing joins may not be updated directly.

For the purpose of the example here, SQL represents a low level of abstraction. End users are not expected to be SQL-literate. SQL is not directly a part of the vocabulary of the problem. Instead, it is used within the implementation of the application, exposing it only to sophisticated tool builders, but hiding it from individuals who must interact with the system on a daily basis.

Take the following scenario: Given an order, one may like to determine the farm's name of the farmer that placed the order. From the perspective of its implementation, carrying out this thread calls for a modest amount of SQL; from the outside perspective, the application client would prefer to stay in the context of C++ and write expressions such as these:

currentOrder.farmer().name()

From the object-oriented perspective of the world, this expression invokes the selector "farmer" to reference the farmer's orders; one can then invoke the selector "name" to return the name of that farmer, as illustrated in the following database query:

```
SELECT      NAME
FROM        ORDERS, FARMERS
WHERE       ORDERS.FARMERID=
            CURRENTORDER.FARMERID
  AND   ORDERS.FARMERID=FARMERS.FARMERID
```

Hiding this secret from the application client allows one to hide all the details of working with SQL. Indeed, mapping an object-oriented view of the world of development projects into a relational one is conceptually straightforward, albeit it in practice involves a lot of tedious details. Thus, there are limitations to using SQL in certain underlying implementations.

Schema Analysis. The list of things presented in the preceding analysis is a start. By taking this list and applying Rumbaugh's rules of thumb for mapping classes and associations, one can provide tables for a database. Rumbaugh's rules of thumb are as follows: (1) each class maps to one or more tables, (2) each many-to-many association maps to a distinct table, and (3) each one-to-many association maps to a distinct table or may be buried as a foreign key. He also suggests that one of three alternatives for mapping superclass/subclass hierarchies to tables: (1) the superclass and each subclass map to a table, (2) superclass attributes are replicated for each table (and each subclass maps to a distinct table), and (3) bring all subclass attributes up to the superclass level (and have one table for the entire superclass/subclass hierarchy) (Booch 1994:398). Thus, for the example in this paper, one must first develop tables that parallel the roles of various groups that interact with the system:

o   FarmerTable
o   SupplierTable
o   OrderAgentTable
o   AccountantTable
o   ShippingAgentTable
o   StockPersonTable
o   ReceivingAgentTable
o   PlannerTable

Next, one must have some tables that deal with the varieties of high-yield seeds products and inventory:

o   ProductTable
o   InventoryTable

Finally, s/he must develop some tables that deal with the warehouse's workflow artifacts:

o   OrderTable
o   PurchaseTable
o   InvoiceTable
o   ParkingOrderTable
o   ShippingLabelTable

Tables for the classes "Report" or "Transaction" are not included because their instances are transitory—i.e. there is no requirement for making them persistent.

Design. To formulate the architecture of the inventory-tracking system suggested here, at least two organizational elements must be addressed: the split in client/server functionality and a strategy for controlling transactions.

Client/Server Architecture. The important thing here is not so much exactly *where* to draw the line between client and server responsibilities but, rather, *how* such a decision is intelligently made. The first step is to focus upon the behavior of each abstraction, to be derived from a use-case analysis of each entity, and only then can one decide where to allocate each abstraction's behavior. After doing this for a few interesting objects, some patterns of behavior will surface; these patterns can then be codified to guide in the allocation of functionality for the remaining abstractions (Booch 1994:400). For example, in considering the behavior of the two classes "Order" and "ProductRecord" in the scenario being examined here, the following operations are applicable:

- o construct
- o setFarmer
- o setOrderAgent
- o addItem
- o removeItem
- o orderID
- o farmer
- o orderAgent
- o numberOfItems
- o itemAt
- o quantityOf
- o totalValue

These services can be mapped directly to a C++ class declaration as follows:

```
// ID types
typedef unsigned int OrderID;

// Type denoting money in local currency
typedef float Money;
```

Next, a declaration is provided for the "Order" class:

```
class Order
public:

        Order ();
        Order(OrderID)
        Order(const Order&);
        ~Order();
        Order& operator=(const Order&);
        int operator==(const Order&) const;
        int operator!=(const Order&) const;
        Void setFarmer(Farmer&);
        void setOrderAgent(Order Agent&);
        void addItem(Product&, unsigned int quantity=1);
        void removeItem(unsigned int index, unsigned int
        quantity=1);

        OrderID orderID() const;
        Farmer& farmer() const;
        OrderAgent& orderAgent() const;
        unsigned int numberOfItems() const;
        Product& itemAt(unsigned int) const;
        unsigned int quantityOf(unsigned int) const;
```

```
Money totalValue() const;

protected:
        ...
};
```

What is evident from the preceding operations is that each of the constructors are given subtly different semantics. The default constructor (Order()) creates a new order object and assigns it a new unique "OrderID" value. Likewise, the copy constructor creates a new order object with a new "OrderID" value; in addition, it also copies the rest of its state from the given argument.

Transaction Mechanism. Client/server computing presupposes a collaboration between client and server, and thus one must have some common mechanism whereby disparate parts of the system can communicates with one another. This calls for three basic types of cooperative processing, according to Berson: pipes, remote procedure calls, and client/server SQL interactions (Booch 1994:405). So far, the last technique (SQL interactions) has been used in the example provided in this paper. However, for a system as the one being proposed for insuring accountability of development projects in African countries, all three techniques must be used at one time or another for reasons of performance or, more pragmatically, that is the convention that certain third-party software to be purchased requires one to use. To maintain a clear and consistent architectural vision, it behooves one to devise a higher-level abstraction that hides her/his choice of communication patterns.

Transactions are the central high-level communications patterns between client and server and among clients. They tend to emerge from a use-case analysis. Each major business function in the inventory-tracking system proposed here can thus, in general, be abstracted as a transaction against the system. Placing an order, acknowledging receipt of new inventory, and updating supplier information are all examples of transactions that are applicable to the system. From the outside, the following operations capture the central abstraction of a transaction's behavior (Booch 1994:406):

o attachOperation
o dispatch
o commit
o rollback
o status

For each transaction, a complete set of operations it is to perform must be identified. This calls for providing member functions such as "attachOperation" for the class "Transaction" that permit other objects to package a collection of SQL statements for execution as one unit.

Indeed, dispatching a transaction is far more complicated when distributed databases are present. As Booch observes:

The simple commit/rollback protocol works if we have to update just one local database, but what if we have to update several databases on distinct servers? The general solution is to use what is called a *two-phase commit protocol*....Under this protocol, an agent first assigns the various parts of the transaction's operations to their appropriate distributed servers; this is the *prepare phase*. If all these participants report that they are ready to commit, then the central transaction that stated this action broadcasts a "commit" action; this is called the *commit phase*. If instead any one server reports back after the prepared phase that it was not ready to commit, then we broadcast a "rollback" so as to back out of the entire distributed transaction. This is largely possible because each instance of "Transaction" encapsulates enough knowledge of its behavior to be able to turn back its original action (1994:406-407).

As the development of the system suggested here is continued, one is likely to find other patterns of transactions that make for suitable sub-classes. For example, "AddTransaction" and "DeleteTransaction" can be invented if one discovers that adding and removing items from certain databases share substantially the same semantics to capture the same behavior. In essence, the base class "Transaction" provides one an open- ended way to construct and dispatch any kind of atomic action. For example, one can write the following in the C++ language (Booch 1994:407-408):

```
class Transaction
public:

        Transaction();
        virtual "Transaction();
        virtual void setOperation(const
        UnboundCollection<SQLStatement>&);
        virtual int dispatch();
        virtual void commit();
        virtual void rollback();
        virtual int status() const;

protected:
    ...
};
```

In its essence, this architectural pattern makes it possible for sophisticated client applications to dispatch raw SQL statements. This power (with its attendant complexity) is hidden by transaction subclasses from simpler clients who only need to perform certain common transactions.

Conclusion

The major conclusion to be drawn from the preceding discussion is that building a client application is a problem of building a GUI intensive program. Nonetheless, the creation of an intuitive and friendly user interface is as much an art as it is a science. In client/server applications such as the one proposed in this paper, it is often the look and feel of the user interface that makes the difference between a widely popular system and one that quickly becomes obsolete. Indeed, building a successful client/server system hinges upon human factors, technical constraints, historical factors, and the personal preferences of members of the development team.

Chapter 3

Functional Programming

Works on the functional approach concentrate as much as possible on a program's logical structure and design rather than simply show how to write code. They provide logical concepts and transparent programs, so that these can be written clearly and quickly. Authors emphasize the notions of function and functional application which relate programming to familiar concepts in the fields of logic and mathematics. In addition to examples, these authors also provide explanations on what programs compute and how one can reason about them (see, for example, Asperti and Guerrini 1998, Banâtre et al. 1991, Burn 1991, Cousineau and Mauny 1998, Kelly 1998, Koopman, Jr. 1990, MacLennan 1990, Milutinovi

1988, Paulson 1991, Peyton Jones et al. 1990, Plasmeijer and van Eekelen 1993, Reade 1989, Traub 1991, Treleanen 1990, and Wikström 1987).

"There is more to functional programming," asserts MacLennan, "than simply pogramming in a functional language." With this in mind, he characterizes *functional programming*, also referred to as *applicative programming* and *value-oriented programming*, as comparable in importance to structured programming. Thus, he argues, functional programming has value as a discipline of thought even in the absence of functional programming languages (MacLennan 1990:iii, 3).

Functional Programming can be treated as a means for reliably deriving programs and as a technique for analyzing programs and proving that they are correct. It can be employed this way, even if the eventual implementation language is a conventional imperative one. In this way, the value of functional programming languages is naturally illustrated. And by emphasizing methodology rather than specific languages, Functional Programming becomes quite useful in software engineering, software prototyping, formal specification, language systems (i.e. compilers and environments), data structure, and algorithm analysis (MacLennan 1990:iii- iv).

Most extant functional languages are experimental in nature—i.e. they are undergoing an evolutionary process, which also suggests that the popular languages of today may be obsolete tomorrow. One exception to this phenomenon is LISP, a quasi-functional language (MacLennan 1990:v). Having been around for 40 years, LISP will likely be around for quite a few more.

Functional Programming has six major advantages that make it pliant for developing computer programs to insure accountability of development projects in African countries, as demonstrated in the examples provided toward the end of this paper. These major advantages, according to Milutinovi (1988:409-410) and MacLennan (1990:3-5), are summarized as follows:

(1) It dispenses with ubiquitous assignment operation.

(2) It encourages thinking at *higher levels of abstraction* by providing mechanisms (higher-order functions) for modifying the behavior of existing programs and combining existing programs.

(3) It provides a paradigm for programming *massively parallel computers*—i.e. computers with hundreds of thousands, perhaps millions of processors.

(4) It is applicable in artificial intelligence (AI).

(5) It is valuable in developing *executable specification* and *prototype implementations*.

(6) Its is connected to computer theory by providing a framework for viewing many of the decidability questions of programming and computers, a simpler framework than that provided by the usual approaches.

A programming language can be divided into two distinct worlds: that of *expressions* and that of *statements*. Higher-level languages have expressions of *various* types, including arithmetic expressions. Expressions usually have a syntax patterned after everyday algebraic notation. Moreover, expressions usually appear on the right hand sides of assignment statements, and in other contexts in which a *value* is required. In its essence, the world of expression includes all those programming language constructs used to yield a *value* through the process of *evaluation*. Higher- level languages also include *statements*, which are of two types: (1) statements that control flow, including conditionals, loops, gotos, and procedure indications; (2) statements that alter the *state* (memory) of the computer, including assignment statements that alter the state of primary memory and input statements that alter the state of secondary memory. And, indeed, the purpose of Functional Programming is the extension of the advantages of expressions to the entire programming language (MacLennan 1990:5-6, 221-293).

In evaluating (i.e. to extract the value of something) pure expressions, the evaluation of one subexpression cannot affect the value of any other subexpression. This allows for *parallel evaluation*—i.e. to evaluate several parts of an expression at the same time (for more on this, see Milutinovi 1988:408-423, MacLennan 1990:8). This independence of evaluation order is best represented drawing an expression as a tree. One can then see that each operation depends only on those directly below it. The evaluation of the subtree can affect only that portion of the tree above itself; it cannot affect subtrees to either the right or the left. When performing an evaluation, one can begin at the leaves, and evaluate the nodes in any order (or in parallel) so long as the inputs to the node have been evaluated before one evaluates the node itself. And no matter what the order of decoration, as long as the structure of the tree is obeyed, the same answer will be derived (Milutinovi 1988:411ff, MacLennan 1990:8-9).

The property of pure expressions, or independence of evaluation order, is referred to as the *Church-Roser property*. This property allows one to construct compilers that choose the evaluation order that makes the best use of machine resources. The ability to do parallel evaluation is one way to employ multiprocessor computers. *Impure* expressions in general lack this property (for details, see MacLennan 1990:10, 398-414).

An arithmetic expression in a fixed context will always evaluate to the same value. And *referential transparency* means that in a fixed context, the replacement of a subexpression by its value is completely independent of the surrounding expression. Thus, after evaluating an expression in a given context, one need not evaluate it again in that context because its value will remain unchanged. Referential transparency can, therefore, be generally characterized as the universal ability to substitute equals for equals. Referential transparency is the outcome of the fact that the arithmetic operators lack memory. Thus, every call of an operator with the same inputs generates the same result. In terms of computer languages, referential transparency allows optimizations such as common subexpression elimination (MacLennan 1990:11-12).

As mathematical notation has evolved over many hundreds of years, it exhibits a number of characteristics that enhances its readability. One such characteristic is *manifest interfaces*—i.e. the input-output connections between a subexpression and its surrounding expression are obviously visible. The notion of manifest interfaces is summarized by MacLennan as follows:

> Expressions can be represented by trees, and the same tree represents both the syntactic structure of the expression and the way that data flows in the expression. Therefore subexpressions that communicate with each other can always be brought into contiguous positions in the tree, or in the written form of the expression. This does not hold in the world of statements; alterable variables permit nonlocal communication. In general the dataflow graph is not a tree, and it may have a very different structure from the syntax tree. Therefore it may not be possible to bring together communicating parts so that their interface is obvious. The structural identity of data dependencies and syntactic dependencies is certainly one of the principal advantages of pure expressions (MacLennan 1990:13-14).

It is therefore only fitting that, as MacLennan points out, Hoare recognizes the following six fundamental principles of structuring (MacLennan 1990:14-15):

(1) *Transparency of meaning*—that the meaning of the whole expression can be understood in terms of the meanings of its subexpressions.

(2) *Transparency of purpose*—that the purpose of each part consists solely in its contribution to the purpose of the whole.

(3) *Independence of parts*—that the meanings of two nonoverlapping parts can be understood completely independently.

(4) *Recursive application*—that arithmetic expressions are built up by the recursive application of uniform rules.

(5) Arithmetic expressions have *narrow interfaces* because each arithmetic operation has only one output and only one or two inputs, and also because each of the inputs and outputs is a conceptually simple value (a number). That is, the interface between the parts is clear, narrow, and well controlled.

(6) *Manifestness of structure*—that the structural relationships between parts of an arithmetic expression are obvious. In Hoare's words, the separation of the parts and their relation to the whole is clearly apparent from their written form.

Two attributes make arithmetic expressions desirable. First, they have structural simplicity—i.e. they are uniformly constructed by the application of arithmetic operations to their arguments. Second, and vital, these operations are *pure functions*—i.e. mathematical mappings from inputs to outputs. This means that the result of an operation hinges only upon its inputs. Also, if a *pure expression* is constructed from pure functions and constants, the value of this expression will always be the same (Milutinovi 1988:429-430, MacLennan 1990:15).

Since the major goal for using Functional Programming is to extend the advantages of arithmetic expressions to the entire programming language, it makes sense to investigate methods for programming with pure expressions. This kind of programming is variously referred to as *value-oriented programming, applicative programming* and, of course, *functional programming*. While many computer scientists use these concepts interchangeably, there are subtle differences between them. Applicative programming is often distinguished from *imperative programming*, a programming approach that employs *imperatives*, or orders. In contrast, the universe of expressions involves the description of *values*, thus the concept value-oriented programming. In applicative programming, programs take the form of *applicative expressions*. Such expressions are either constants (literal, e.g., '2,' or named, e.g., ''), or expressions made up entirely of the *application* of pure functions to their arguments, which are also applicative expressions (MacLennan 1990:16).

Applicative programming possesses a single fundamental built-in syntactic construct: i.e. the application of a function to its argument. This construct is so basic that it is usually represented implicitly, by juxtaposition, rather than explicitly, by some symbol. Consequently, 'sin ' stands for the application of the function named 'sin' to the value named ',' and 'sum $(x, 1)$' stands for the application of the function named 'sum' to the pair composed of the value named 'x' and the number 1 (MacLennan 1990:17, 36).

Thus, to program with functions, one needs to first consider the ways in which functions can be defined. Mathematically, a function is simply a set of input-output pairs. As a consequence, one method of defining a function is the enumeration of its pairs. *Enumerative definition*—i.e. the exhibition of the input-output correspondence for each possible input—is practical only when the function has a small, finite domain. However, not many functions can be defined by enumeration. Instead, functions are commonly defined as *composition* of already defined functions; this is referred to as *definition by composition* (MacLennan 1990:17, 67, 114-115).

If one knows how to apply the primitive functions, then all s/he needs to do with other function application is just substitution. This process is *domain-independent*—i.e. the same regardless whether one is dealing with functions of numbers, functions of characters, functions of trees, etc. Often, the definition of a function cannot be expressed simply as a composition of other functions. Instead, there exist several different cases, each with a different composition. Sometimes, one may wish to define a function in terms of an infinite number of compositions. But since one cannot write down an infinite number of cases, this method of function definition is useful only if there is some regularity, some unifying principle, among the cases that permits her/him to generate the unwritten cases from the written ones. This is the objective of a *recursive definition*, one in which the thing defined is defined in terms of itself (MacLennan 1990:18-19, 168-171, 294- 297).

Finally, a distinction should be made between *explicit* and *implicit* definitions of functions. Explicit definitions have the advantage that they can be interpreted as *rewrite-rules*—i.e. rules that tell one how to replace a class of expressions by another. According to MacLennan, the notion of explicit definition can be extended to sets of *simultaneous equations* as follows: "A set of variables is explicitly defined by a set of equations provided that both (1) the equations are individually explicit and (2) they can be ordered so that no equation uses on its right-hand side a variable defined earlier in the list" (MacLennan 1990:20). An implicit definition, on the other hand, is characterized by an equation in which it appears on both sides. However, variables can also be defined implicitly by sets of *simultaneous equations*, and implicit definitions in which the variables do not appear on both sides of the equations do exist (MacLennan 1990:21).

Moreover, as MacLennan asks, "What does a functional program look like?" To this question, he responds, a major portion of such a program would hinge on the definition of functions. Functional programming languages differ greatly in their syntactic styles, mainly due to the fact that most of them are *experimental* languages, one of the purposes of which is to experiment with notations. However, underneath the syntactic idiosyncrasies, most of these languages are based on the lambda calculus. Ladin is credited with inventing the concept *syntactic sugar* to describe the abbreviations and syntactic conventions adopted by the languages to make programming in the lambda calculus more convenient. The idea is that "a little bit of syntactic sugar helps you swallow the lambda calculus." And since most functional languages are just sugared versions of the lambda calculus, it is usually easy to translate between them. Thus, the functional programming techniques one learns in one language, say, lambda calculus, can be transferred to other languages, e.g., abstract calculus (MacLennan 1990:26, 350-351, 398-399, 421-470). Let us take a look at some of the languages used in functional programming.

Programming Languages

Languages used for functional programming have been classified into two general categories: (1) procedural or imperative languages and (2) declarative and applicative languages. A discussion of these languages ensues. This will allow one to see functional programming as comprising of descriptions of values, properties, methods, problems and solutions. Thus, the role of the machine is simply to speed up the manipulation and evaluation of these descriptions to provide solutions to particular problems.

Procedural/Imperative Languages are based on the idea that instructions are to be carried out like a recipe. The instructions incrementally transform a storage, comprised of cells, by updating the contents of the cells to achieve some overall effect. An assignment such as the following:

$$X:=X+1$$

is usually perceived to be an instruction employed to up the contents of the storage cell associated with storage variable X by adding 1 to the current contents (Reade 1989:2).

According to Reade (1989:2), procedural/imperative languages have evolved from a von Neumann model of sequential machines and their control mechanisms have emerged as abstractions from the use of a program counter to locate the next instruction and to perform jumps by updating the program counter.

Reade also points out that the main outcome of having variables which refer directly to storage cells is that the programmer has the responsibility of organizing her/his use and re-use to hold different values, and of distributing large values across many cells by using arrays, for example. The programmer, Reade adds, is having to do several things at the same time, namely:

(1)   describe what is to be computed;

(2)   organize the computation sequencing into small steps;

(3)   organize memory management during the computation (1989:2).

Conventional programming languages—e.g., FORTRAN, COBOL, ALGOL 60, ALGOL 68, Pascal, C, Clu, Modula, and Ada—essentially employ assignment statements as the basic construct around which the control abstractions of sequencing, branching, looping, etc. are developed (Reade 1989:2). Let us take a further look at some of these procedural/imperative languages.

FORTRAN, an acronym for FORmula TRANslation, was developed because of the need to get out of the dependency on machine structure (now called "Assembly Language"). FORTRAN allowed earlier users of machines to employ a set of very elementary instructions. While the effect of FORTRAN may seem a limited step, it nevertheless changed fundamentally the very nature of programming by separating the structure of the programming language from the structure of the machine.

This separation hinged upon the idea of a **compiler**—i.e. a program that translates programs written by a user into programs that can be executed by machines (Cousineau and Mauny 1998:3).

COBOL, or Common Business Oriented Language, was until the end of the 1980s the most widespread commercial programming language because it is a common, standard, machine-independent language; it is business- oriented, making it suitable for business applications; and it is English-like or self-documenting. COBOL has been widely replaced by C because the former is rigid—i.e. it is verbose with strict programming rules; non- mathematical and, thus, not suitable for scientific computations; and non- interactive, since it is batch-oriented.

PL/I, or Programming Language/I, was the first high-level language that permitted structured programming but was still a very flexible language. It combines the scientific computation aspects of FORTRAN, the file- handling capability of COBOL, and superior text-handling capabilities. Because of these features, PL/I supports a large number of statements (McKeown 1988:533).

BASIC was a simple language, in which programs could be written with as few as seven statement types. As an interpreted language, BASIC was easy for students to use because errors were signaled to the user during execution. The current versions of BASIC are far different from the earlier ones. Many new commands have been added to transform the language from a beginner's instructional language into one that can be used to write commercial software (McKeown 1988:535-536).

ALGOL, or ALGOrithmic Language, of which PASCAL and ADA are remote descendants, was the basis for significant progress after FOR- TRAN. ALGOL makes it possible to refine studies about different modes for passing parameters as well as the introduction of richer data structures (Cousineau and Mauny 1998:3).

APL, or A Programming Language, is a special purpose language employed for mathematical and scientific formulae. With special symbols such as Greek alphabets and overstrike characters, APL can accomplish in one line what other languages might take 10 lines to do. It is also an interpreted language that is easy to utilize. It is nevertheless difficult to decipher because of its special symbols and compactness (McKeown 1988:540)..

Pascal is widely used for teaching introductory computer science. This language's popularity is due to the fact that it must be written in a manner that meets accepted programming standards. Consequently, many students do not learn to write properly designed programs. Pascal has a clean, bloc-structure approach to programming, which makes the language easy to use and learn. It is also a **strongly typed language**, meaning that all variable names must be declared at the beginning of the program. The computer must be informed what each variable name stands for—the type of quantity, whole numbers, decimal numbers, text, etc. Thus, the user must think through the program before writing it. Pascal programs must have a PRO-GRAM statement that names the program, a VAR statement that comes before the variable declarations, and a BEGIN statement that defines the beginning of the actual program logic. The program always ends with an END statement. Other BEGIN and END statements are used to define blocks of material within the main program (McKeown 1988:536-537). Modula looks much like Pascal, but it is used for systems development.

C exists not so much because it represents obvious progress but rather because it supports an an innovation application with respect to UNIX (Cousineau and Mauny 1998:4). C is a mid-level language with the power of a high-level language (PASCAL or FORTRAN, for example) and the flexibility of a low-level language such as assembly language. Thus C is small, yet powerful, fast and efficient. With C, one can build complex data structures as in high-level languages and s/he cam manipulate individual bits of data in memory as with assembly language. It is employed for such diverse projects as spreadsheets, word processors, graphics, operating systems, and compilers for other languages.

Ada was developed for the United States Department of Defense so that all military software should be written in the same language. Much like Pascal, Ada is a structured language. However, it has many more features than Pascal, because of the tremendous amount of software developed for military computers (McKeown 1988:542).

Smalltalk is the predecessor of Apple's desktop metaphor, which uses menus with icons to help the user choose an option. It is based on the notion that the computer works by sending messages vis-a-vis the idea of **object-oriented language** (McKeown 1988:541).

LOGO is probably the easiest language to use. Preschool children learn how to move the special LOGO graphics cursor around on the screen to trace patterns. The cursor, referred as a **turtle**, is moved via simple geometric commands. Using other commands such as GROW and EDIT, one can draw sophisticated figures on the screen, and at the same time learn the concept of programming logic. With more advanced commands, one can use LOGO for non-graphic programming tasks similar to those performed by other high-level languages. A user of LOGO can also generate new commands by combining available commands to meet her/his needs (McKeown 1988:540-541).

PILOT (Program Inquiry Learning Or Teaching) was developed for instructional situations. PILOT replaced BASIC for this purpose because the latter has become a very sophisticated language (McKeown 1988:541).

Forth was originally created by an astronomer to control telescopes. It is now a very fast, high-level language that has a small, but developed, following of users. Unlike other languages, Forth uses **reverse Polish notation (RPN)** like the one used on Hewlette-Packard calculators. In PRN, 3 4 + 5 X means to add 3 and 4 to get 7, and then to multiply this value by 5 to obtain. Thus, Forth has allowed programmers to significantly increase their productivity (McKeown 1988:541).

Declarative/Applicative Languages are very high level media that are based on expressions. Their design is influenced by clear mathematical understanding of descriptions, as opposed to particular machine details. They also involve alternative means for describing data values and calculations, not just certain facilities like assignment statements (Reade 1989:4).

Reade suggests four major properties that a declarative/applicative language must exhibit. They are as follows (Reade 1989:4-5):

(1) It should be **expressive** so that descriptions of problems, situations, methods and solutions are not too difficult to write. On the other hand, it should have a simple, uniform basis so that it is not difficult to understand.

(2) It should be **extensible**, allowing the user to extend the language easily from a simple basis to suit particular needs rather than having a large collection of primitive constructs.

(3) It should **protect** users from making too many errors as far as possible (for example, by not allowing inconsistent uses of descriptions). It should be possible to write programs with the language which run efficiently on currently available machines.

(4) It should be mathematically **elegant** in order to allow for mathematical support in the major programming activities. More specifically, analysis, design, specification, implementation, abstraction and especially reasoning (derivations of consequences and properties) are becoming more and more formal activities. Declarative languages are usually generated from mathematical principles. After all, a large part of mathematical activity has been centered on describing and reasoning about complex objects and it would be unwise to ignore this legacy of notations and concepts when programming.

Let us take a look at some of these declarative/applicative languages.

PROLOG, based on first order logic, is an outgrowth of lambda calculus. It is used to give programming a healthy theoretical basis. First order logic was employed to develop systems of proof to establish the correctness of programs formally with respect to their specifications (Cousineau and Mauny 1998:4).

LISP (for LISt Processing) is completely functional, since it does not contain any imperative features. Its objects are symbolic expressions that are either atoms (strings of characters—letters, digits or other special symbols) or lists (sequences of atoms or lists, separated by spaces and bracketed by parentheses). It also offers a few primitive functions from which it is possible to construct new functions (Banâtre et al. 1991:30-31).

LISP has been the basis of some essential innovations. It was created for the purpose of non-numerical applications in artificial intelligence (AI), proving to be extremely innovative. For instance, it fostered the adoption of data structures that were simultaneously rich and simple, facilitating the representation of all sorts of symbolic objects, including LISP programs themselves. It promoted the systematic use of recursion, supported allocation and automatic recovery of memory, and fostered interaction. However, its high inefficiency in performance made LISP somewhat obscure during its infancy. It was not until the 1980s that increasing memory capacity and efficient compilers made it feasible to develop large scale applications in LISP or to distribute LISP applications like Macsyma, a system for computer algebra and symbolic computation, more widely (Cousineau and Mauny 1998:3-4).

ML, or Meta Language, is a strongly typed and polymorphic functional language. It entails a sequence of expressions that contain definitions of variables (in the LISP sense) and function applications. ML was originally designed as the command language in the Edinburgh Logic of Computable Functions (LCF) system, a system used to prove properties in a theory of program called PP-Lambda (Banâtre et al. 1991:33). In other words, LCF is a system used to prove the correctness of programs. However, as Paulson (1991:9-10) notes, ML, just as FORTRAN, LISP and PROLOG, is today being used in diverse problem areas, and several universities have adopted it as a teaching language. In research, ML is being applied to formal methods, artificial intelligence, the construction of ML compilers, etc.

CAML is a dialect of ML. CAML seems to be a reasonable compromise between rigor and realism. With an essentially functional spirit, the language allows users to employ conceptual tools close to the mathematical tradition to specify and verify programs. It also allows for a programming vision that is less tangled up in technical details than if a user had chosen a language in more current use. Moreover, CAML is a realistic language that supports imperative programming when it is necessary. A version known as CAML LIGHT can be used in micro-processors.

LOP (for Logic Programming) was developed to provide an input language based on full first-order logic for parallel inference systems. More features were later added to increase the ease of programming in general, and towards a specification and programming language for parallel systems in particular. The syntax of LOP provides basically two notations, which can also be mixed within one program. One variant is similar to PROLOG notation, using the reverted conditional ":-" to separate the head of a clause from its tail. The other variant, which facilitates a more concise description at the cost of reduced execution control, makes it possible to use multiple literals in the head of a clause (Treleaven 1990:280-281).

FP2, or Functional Parallel Programming, is a functional language that is based entirely on operations of *terms*. In it, values are represented as typed terms. The types are term algebras on sets of constructor names. Also, one can define first-order functions with term-rewriting rules (Treleaven 1990:263).

K-LEAF syntax is based on Horn Clause Logic with Equality, which extends pure PROLOG to express *non-terminating conditional term rewriting systems with constructors*. Given a set of V of variables, C of constructors, F of functions, and P of predicates, a K-LEAF program consists of a set of clauses whose syntax is defined by a specific grammar (Treleaven 1990:176).

IDEAL extends K-LEAF with the possibility to handle lambda abstractions, key for defining higher-order functions or predicates. In addition, IDEAL programs are constrained to be well *polymorphic systems* (Treleaven 1990:177).

POOL, or Parallel Object-Oriented Language, is used to execute the body of an object, providing each object with an independent activity. Different objects execute in parallel, and they may interact by explicitly sending and answering of messages. Within an object, all activities are strictly sequential; the presence of parallelism inside objects would cause problems by necessitating additional mechanisms to synchronize processes. Thus, POOL objects can be created dynamically, the data they contain can be modified, and each object can have its own independent internal activity (Treleaven 1990:52).

VIM is a product-rule intermediate language that can be used to express the relational algebra and even transitive closure by recursive rules. A VIM program is a set of VIM rules which produces by saturation all possible facts from the facts in the database and rules. The output is a set of deduced facts. VIM is rationally complete, and it can also express recursion. Thus, this language is essential because recursive rules can be used in sequential languages (Treleaven 1990:149-150).

Miranda is a straightforward commercial implementation of a lazy functional programming language that utilizes combinator graph reduction. This language is perceived by programmers as being slow and unsophisticated. Nonetheless, Miranda makes a good baseline for comparisons among graph reducers, since it forms a widely available lower bound on expected performance (Koopman, Jr. 1990:9). In addition, the language is equipped with many features such as rich type system that helps the user to develop meaningful, elegant and compact programs (Plasmeijer and von Eekelen 1993:38).

A Miranda program has two parts: (1) the **script**, which is a collection of declarations; and (2) **initial expression** which is to be evaluated. The declarations in the scripts are either function definitions or type declarations (Plasmeijer and von Eekelen 1993:38).

CEDAR is a strongly typed language of the PASCAL family. CEDAR is made up of separately compiled modules. These modules are of two types. The first are the *interface* modules which are a specification of the data abstraction represented by the module. And the second are the *implementation* modules which contain the concrete representation of the data abstraction and the implementation of the functions operating on this abstraction. These two kinds of modules are akin to the definition package and the representation package in ADA (Banâtre et al. 1991:4).

In addition, CEDAR offers facilities for process definitions and activation. Synchronization is achieved by using the concept of monitors. Features also exist for exception handling and for safe memory management. Since the language provides automatic storage management, the programmer does not have to specifically allocate and deallocate objects with the risk of creating invalid references (Banâtre 1991:4-5).

TIGRE is a language used to define a low-level, abstract implementation of combinators for the TIGRE abstract machine. Consequently, it requires the property of concisely defining the actions that are needed to process a particular combinator, together with the property of efficient mapping onto a variety of commercially available hardware platforms. TIGRE is defined in terms of resource names and abstract machine instructions. The syntax employed is comprised of either a one- or two-operand register/memory based instruction format. And the resources controlled by the language include the interpretive pointer *ip*, computational scratchpad registers, the spine stack, and heap memory (Koopman, Jr. 1990:26-27).

Lambda Calculus as a programming language uses typical data structures of functional languages, including infinite lists, which are encoded in the lambda calculus. Demonstrated in this language is the evaluation of recursive functions (Paulson 1991:315-316). In lambda calculus, a programmar can write down expressions (**lambda terms** or **lambda expressions**) in which anonymous functions can be defined together with the expressions on which these functions are applied. Moreover, there are evaluation rules called **reduction rules** (or **rewrite rules**) defined in the calculus that specify how a lambda expression can be transformed into an equivalent lambda expression, i.e. an expression denoting the same value (Plasmeijer and van Eekelen 1993:80).

In sum, a major advantage of functional programming is that, much like elementary algebra, it simplifies the transformation of implicit into explicit definitions. This is critical in developing computer programs for insuring accountability of development projects in African countries because formal specifications of software definitions often take the form of implicit definitions, whereas explicit definitions are usually easy to convert to programs. Thus, Functional Programming can provided a way to go from formal specifications of various aspects of development projects to programs satisfying those specifications, as the following examples of the structure of functional programs illustrate.

Examples of the Structure of a Functional Program

First to be considered is the matter of program entry. Since it is impractical to type in function and data definitions afresh in every terminal session, most functional programming systems thus allow a file to be loaded that contains function and data definitions. Once loaded, these definitions can be invoked interactively from the terminal (Milutinovi 1988:423-424, MacLennan 1990:33). For instance, suppose the file 'payrolls' contains the source commands shown here:

> **let** $C (n, k)$=fac n / [fac k x fac $(n-k)$]
> **let** fac 0 1
>> Fac $n=n$ x fac $(n-1)$, if $n > 0$

(Of course, a real program file tends to contain hundreds of function definitions such as these). One cannot command the functional language system to read this file by typing

```
6 do 'payrolls'
  payrolls done
6
```

The system will interpret the commands in the file just as if they were typed from the terminal.

Many development projects require large data sets; one certainly does not want to have to type these interactively. One solution is to write input files in the form of data definition commands. For example, a file called input might look like this:

```
let input=<
(4321  ('Bangura',    'Piere'),     42.2),
(4578, ('Sulaiman',   'Sheriff'),   35.9),

      .           .         .       .
      :           :         :       :
(5326  ('Sorie',     'Petit'),      52.4)>
```

This file can be loaded in the usual way:

```
6 do 'input'
  input done.
6
```

This approach requires that the file be in the form of a legal data definition, which may be inconvenient. It also does not address the problem of *writing* files so that they can be employed by other programs.

A more general approach to the problem of files is to include a construct in the language that allows external file names to be treated as global names for sequences. Thus, wherever one employs the expression, say, **file** 'OldPersonnel,' s/he is referring to the contents of the file called OldPersonnel. For example, the application

process_updates (**file** 'OldPersonnel', **file** 'Updates')

passes the file OldPersonnel and Updates to the function process-updates (which is assumed to produce a new master file). The result of this application can be stored into the file system by using and external file name on the left of a data definition:

6 **let file** 'NewPersonnel' =process_updates (**file** 'OldPersonnel', **file** 'Updates')
NewPersonnel defined
6

This *defines* the file NewPersonnel to be the result of applying process_updates to the files OldPersonnel and Updates.

For another example, suppose one has a Pascal compiler on a file called Pascal and Pascal program on a file called prog.personnel. S/he might compile it, producing object code prog.exe and listing prog.lst, as follows:

6**do** 'Pascal'
Pascal done
6**let** (**file** 'prog.exe', **file** 'prog.lst')=Pascal (**file** 'prog.personnel')

Here, it is assumed that Pascal is also the name of the compiler function defined by the file Pascal.

Finally, as MacLennan points out, it is often convenient to compile a program so that it can be invoked from the operating system, with file names provided as parameters. To accomplish this, one needs to compile the functional program as a batch program—i.e. a file containing a collection of function and data declarations followed by a single expression to be evaluated. The structure of the batch-program file might look like the following (MacLennan 1990:34-35):

> **let** process_updates (*x, y*)= ...body of process-updates...
> **Let** summarize S= ...body of an auxiliary function...
>
> $\vdots$
>
> other function and data definitions
>
> $\vdots$
>
> process_updates (input1, input2)

In the preceding example, 'input1' and 'input2' are predefined names that are automatically bound to the input file(s) passed to the program by the operating system. The value of the expression 'process_updates (input1, input2)' is employed to provide the values of the output file(s) whose names were passed to the program by the operating system.

Conclusion

Indeed, from the preceding discussion, it is quite obvious that Functional Programming can be useful in developing programs for insuring accountability of development projects in African countries because of two considerations that make the technique vital in Computer Science. These are: (1) the role of mathematics and (2) the advantages of functions. A further discussion of these considerations is necessary.

First, computation is the mechanical manipulation of symbolic structures. Thus, mathematics, the principal tool for symbolic manipulation, must retain a role in the science of computation. And since Functional Programming is essentially programming in mathematics, mathematical tools are especially applicable to functional programs dealing with project development.

Second, significant advantages to the use of functions stem from the fact that applicative (pure) expressions are *referentially unambiguous*—they possess a unique *referent*. This is because applicative expressions, like ideal development projects, are built up from (unambiguous) constants by the recursive application of single-valued functions.

Chapter 4

Parallel Programming

The development in computer technology has concentrated on the production of newer and faster serial computers, leading to efficient and relatively cheaper machines. Consequently, the trend in hardware technology has focused on increased miniaturization, speed and reliability. Inevitably, factors like speed of the propagation signals, the physical limit of miniaturization and the number of modules that can be packed into a certain area of a chip have become crystallized. Moreover, there has been a decrease in the cost per element which has stimulated the use of more elements connected to parallel programming. Thus, for both technological and economic reasons, one sees in various publications on parallel programming trends toward even higher degrees of parallelism as a means of improving performance (e.g., Alexandrov and Megson 1999, Babb 1988, Bauer 1992, Bernstein and Lewis 1993, Brawer 1989, Carriero and Gelernter 1990, Chanda and Misra 1988, Cok 1991, Jamieson et al. 1987, Kaufmann and Smarr 1993, Lakshmivarahan and Dhall 1990, Osterhaug 1989, Ragsdale 1991, Reilly 1990, Szymanski 1991, Wilkinson and Allen 1999, and Williams 1990).

Despite this upsurge in contemporary works on parallelism, the beginnings of this programming approach, as Kaufmann and Smarr (1993:41) recount, can be traced back to the late 1960s, as an important innovation in computer design was carried out at the University of Illinois under the direction of Dan Slotnick. The Illinois computer scientists and engineers developed the ILLIAC IV machine. Once built by the Burroughs Corporation, this machine became the first massively parallel computer. Unlike the STAR 100, ASC, and Cray-1, which had single vector units, the ILLIAC IV had 64 identical scalar computers that operated in parallel, each with its own processing unit and local memory.

Accountability of development projects in African countries can be enhanced greatly by employing parallel programming because in a parallel computer, a particular nationwide project's computation can be divided among the processors, which can complete the task much faster than a single central processing unit (CPU) laboring in isolation. This assertion is supported by the following example provided by Kaufmann and Smarr:

> Suppose, for instance, that 100 pairs of numbers are to be multiplied on a parallel machine with two processors. One processor might calculate the multiplication of the first 50 pairs of numbers while the other processor calculates the multiplication of the other 50 pairs. As the calculation proceeds, the processors march forward in lock step, so that they all fetch from memory, add a pair of numbers, and return to memory simultaneously (1993:41).

In essence, a parallel computer can achieve considerably more speed than a strict von Neuman architecture. The rest of this chapter provides a brief introduction to parallel programming, people as processors, machines as processors, and an example of a comparison of programming models of parallel processing for development projects in African countries.

Brief Introduction to Parallel Programming

As Justo points out, parallel processing is not a new concept, and the first ideas can be traced back to 1842 with the work of Charles Babbage when he stated the following:

> When a long series of identical computations is to be performed, such as those required for the formation of numerical tables, the machine can be brought in to play so as to give several results at the same time, which will greatly abridge the whole amount of the process (Justo 1996:1).

Justo further notes that the idea also appeared in the very first issues of the *Communications of ACM* published in 1958, as follows:

> We know that the so-called parallel computers are somewhat faster than the serial ones, and that no matter how faster we make access and arithmetic serially, we can do correspondingly better in parallel. However access and arithmetic speeds seem to be approaching a definite limit...Does this mean that digital speeds are reaching a limit, that digital computation of multi- variate differential systems must accept it, and that predicting tomorrow's weather must require more than one day? Not if we have truly-parallel machines, with say, a thousand instruction register (Justo 1996:1).

The advent and following popularity of the electronic computer made it imperative to think *sequentially* if problems were to be solved. This was due to the Von Neumann principle—i.e. the computer executes one statement and then control passes to the next statement. That way, the algorithms that represented the solution to a program were forced to fit a mould dictated by the computer that was to solve the problem. Consequently, non-sequential computers can never be fully utilized if this mould cannot be broken (Williams 1990:1, Chandy and Misra 1988:8).

A *shared-memory multiprocessor* computer—i.e. a single computer with two or more CPUs—is frequently used for parallel programs to derive full performance benefit. In this case, all the CPUs would share a single pool of memory, and every processor can access any byte of memory in the same amount of time (see Cok 1991:26, Jamieson et al. 1987:395, Babb II 1988:43-399, Osterhaug 1989:5-20, Ragsdale 1991:8). Indeed, several general-purpose, shared-memory multiprocessors with more than ten CPUs exist (for examples, see Brawer 1989:27-39).

Multiprocessor computers can be utilized for general-purpose time-sharing as well as for computer-intensive applications. A multiprocessor will not be any more or less difficult to use than a uniprocessor when a user only runs "canned" programs or creates only single stream (i.e. non-parellelized, programs that employ only a single CPU at a time) applications. Each program runs on its own processor, if possible, when single-stream programs are used on a multiprocessor computer. Each processor will effectively share a smaller number of programs than would be the case on a uniprocessor when the number of programs becomes greater than the number of processors (Brawer 1989:2).

In addition to running completely isolated programs, parallel processing is useful for calculating a number of nearly independent, but communicating, calculations. Some of these are independent compilation of files, Monte Carlo simulations of trajectories, database management systems, sorting, enumerating relatively independent paths, exploring a maze, and parallel I/O (refer to Brawer 1989:2, Wilkinson and Allen 1999, Bauer 1992).

Another kind of parallelism is the apportionment of what is normally perceived to be an indivisible calculation among many processors. To illustrate the general idea, Brawer provides the following example of a program which contains a loop over a variable i in which the statement

$$x (i) = a (i) + b (i)$$

is executed within the loop. If this program were written in a way suitable for parallel processing, Brawer proposes that one of the processors might execute the statement

$$x (1) = a (1) + b (1)$$

while, *at the same time*, another may do

$$x (2) = a (2) + b (2)$$

a third might do x (3), and so forth. Brawer concludes that, since different iterations of the loop are executed simultaneously, the work can be completed more rapidly than it it were done by a single CPU (Brawer 1989:2-3).

According to Lakshmivarahan and Dhall (1990:5-8), a general model for the study of parallel computation is often referred to as a *paracomputer*. It is comprised of a set of identical general purpose processors, *Pi*, $1 \le i \le p$, each with its own local memory. For its own computations, each processor uses the local memory that holds the programs like a scratch pad. The assumption is that each processor knows its own index. The processors can run either synchronously or asynchronously. In a synchronous model, all the processors run identical programs, albeit may operate on different segments of data given their own index. In an asynchronous scheme, each processor may run on different sets of programs. The processors communicate with each other by writing into and reading from the shared memory with an infinite number of memory cells. In a given scheme, each processor may either perform some computation or read from or write into the shared memory. By limiting the ways in which various processes write into and read from the shared memory, Lakshmivarahan and Dhall delineate a variety of successively weaker models, as follows (1990:8):

(a) *Models with Concurrent Read and Concurrent Write (CRCW.) Capability:* In this case simultaneous reading from and writing into the same memory location by different processors is allowed. We can further subdivide this model depending on the way in which write conflict is resolved. When multiple writes occur, one way to resolve the conflict is to let the processor with the least index, for example, write. This is called the *priority write CRCW* model. However, in the design of parallel algorithms for this model, the proof of correctness becomes much less involved if we require that all processors write the *same* quantity when simultaneous write takes place. This latter requirement is often called the *common* write rule, and the model with this requirement is often called the *common write CRCW* model.

(b) *Models with Concurrent Read but Exclusive Write (CREW) Capability:* These models, while permitting simultaneous reading from a given memory cell by more than one processor, do *not* permit writing into a given cell by more than one processor. Thus, like the CRCW model, this model also allows fetch conflicts. This model is also known as P-RAM (for parallel random access memory) model.

(c) *Models with Exclusive Read and Exclusive Write (EREW) capability:* In this model, neither simultaneous writing into nor reading from a given memory cell is allowed. This model is also known as P-RAC (for parallel random access computer) and is more realistic, since this does not permit fetch conflicts while restricting the writing to only one processor.

In addition, Lakshmivarahan and Dhall point out that another class of models that have received considerable attention is referred to as *combinational* or *Boolean circuit models*. "A Boolean circuit C is a finite, directed acyclic graph with nodes classified into two groups: *input* and *operation* nodes" (1990:9).

There are two types of parallelism. The first, *coarse-grained* parallelism, involves nearly independent tasks such as database management, parallel I/O, and Monte Carlo simulations of trajectories. The second, *fine-grained* parallelism, involves different iterations of a loop that are executed by different processors. Thus, as to be expected, fine-grained parallel programming is generally more difficult to do than coarse-grained programming, albeit both types of parallelism depend on exactly the same principles (refer to Brawer 1989:2, Bauer 1992:7-10, Chandy and Misra 1988:85-86).

In addition, Bauer (1992: 3-6) suggests two categories within which the underlying algorithm of a parallelized block can be placed. The first is *homogenous* parallelization—in which the same code is applied to multiple data elements. The second is *heterogenous* parallelization—in which multiple codes are applied to multiple data elements. Homogenous parallelization, on the one hand, is possible when the work to be accomplished by the algorithm can be separated into identical subtasks, each working on a portion of the total task. The obvious candidates for homogenous parallelization are loops made up of a finite number of iterations. Heterogenous parallelization, on the other hand, is possible when the task to be performed by the algorithm is spread over a larger number of *different* subtasks, each of which works a discrete portion of the total algorithm. A candidate for heterogenous parallelization is an algorithm that has multiple independent components in which each can be executed separately.

Thus, as Ragsdale points out, a loosely-coupled parallel system provides three major advantages (1991:3-4):

(1) It is flexible. Nodes with different types of processors can be used to adapt the system to specialized problems.

(2) It is cost-effective. Parallel processing can significantly reduce the processing time for large computation-intensive problems. While some systems use specifically designed components, others further reduce costs by using existing technology wherever possible.

(3) It is easily scalable. Loosely-coupled systems are easy to expand, and you can also run several smaller problems concurrently.

Indeed, it is because a distributed-memory parallel computer operates like a large corporation with divisions distributed around the world that makes it ideal for insuring accountability in development projects in African countries. Each project has its own goals, but all projects must work in close communication to operate a successful development program.

Several methods exist to measure the performance of both parallel computers and parallel algorithms. The peak performance of a machine is usually expressed in units of millions of instructions executed per second (MIPS) or millions of floating point operations executed per second (MFLOPS). However, in practice, the realizable performance may be far lower than the peak performance. The actual realizable performance is a function of the match between the algorithms and the architecture. The match is better understood by benchmarking (Lakshmivarahan and Dhall 1990:18).

People as Processors

To understand the notion of people as processors, William's example is quite instructive. As she suggests, consider that there are a number of people available to help with calculating the maximum value of the sums of subsequences. She then asks the question: Will one's algorithm help her/him to utilize these people? At this point, she suggests, there are a number of questions that should be asked as follows (Williams 1990:2):

(1)   How many people?
(2)   Where are they?
(3)   How bright are they?
(4)   How are they going to know what to do?
(5)   How are they going to let us know they have finished and any results they have achieved?

Williams then suggests that one considers where there is a large class of students (almost an infinite supply of people). Then the sequence could be displayed on a board at the front of the room and different students could be asked to calculate each of the possible subsequences. When a student completes her/his task, s/he puts a hand up in the air. When all students doing the calculations complete their tasks, one at random is asked for her/his sum. Then the class is asked if anyone has a greater answer. If no one does, then that sum is the answer; otherwise, only the group with larger sums are considered and one is chosen at random and cycled round until the maximum subsequence is isolated (Williams 1990:2-3).

A number of minor variations can be used with the preceding example, according to Williams. For example, she notes, once two students have calculated their sums, one can compare for the greater, even though other students are still calculating (care is needed not to distract those performing mental arithmetic). She points out that, if there are less students than sums to be performed, then once a students completes her/his calculation s/he can be given another sum to perform while there are calculations to be done (clever scheduling helps here: allocation of the longest sums first will reduce the chance of a bottleneck created by the most difficult sum being given as the least calculation and everyone else waiting for that student to finish). Thus, Williams concludes that for any given group of people, it is possible to ask if this is a realistic task to set these people or if this is the best algorithm to use given this group (Williams 1990:3-4).

Machines as Processors

Parallel processing machines are constructed from a number of processors that conform to a variety of models. These models, each comprising a number of processing elements, have been classified in a number of ways. Williams (1990:4) identifies the following five distinct hardware models:

(1) Sequential
(2) Processor array
(3) Pipeline processors
(4) Shared memory
(5) Message passing

These models, according to Williams, are also represented in software.

Williams further notes that, while there are proposals for many other models of parallelism, the preceding five categories can always be mapped into from any other models. Thus, these are the five basic models. She adds that the other most popular models are:

(6) Object-oriented
(7) Functional

Williams also points out that other models have been proposed, some encompassing various aspects of the preceding ones to meet specific applications. These are briefly:

(1)   The sequential model is the conventional model

(2)   The professor array reflects lots of *stupid* processors obeying a controller

(3)   The pipeline is a line of specialist processors that information is passed down

(4)   A shared memory model represents many processors working on a common pool of data

(5)   A message-passing processor represents many processors working together but communicating according to a well-defined protocol

(6)   Object-oriented models consider the data more important than the processes

(7)   A functional model describes the relationship between the input data and the output data (Williams 1990:4).

Indeed, as Williams cautions, the preceding are merely thumbnail sketches and should be read with a pinch of salt! An alternative description of a farming dilemma, also amenable to the application of salt, is now presented.

A Comparison of Programming Models for Parallel Processing (or a Farming Drama)

Consider the following scenario:

An African government's store manager has just supplied high-yield coffee seeds to a farming community; all that remains is to clear the fields, till the soil, plant the seeds, tend the coffee, control for pests, harvest the coffee when it is fully grown, load and deliver the coffee for sale to the government marketing board. Given the models discussed in the preceding section, there are a number of different solutions to this problem, depending on the number of workers (processors) available. There are also a number of ways in which a solution can be described.

(1) A Sequential Model Using One Processor:

o The government store manager supplies the high-yield coffee seeds
o While the farmers clear the fields, till the soil, plant the seeds, tend the coffee, control for pests, harvest the coffee, load and deliver the coffee for sale to the government marketing board

According to Bernstein and Lewis, a sequential model is one in which no more than one operation is executing at any time, and that a computer is sequential if no more than one control point can be serviced at a time. In short, the primitive computer with a single control unit is sequential. But that even though the primitive computer with a single control unit is simple, it is also inefficient. For example, an I/O transfer might involve mechanical motion, which is slow compared to electronic speeds; hence, during the time it takes to execute an I/O transfer, considerable computation could be performed. A common approach for increasing the efficiency of such a computer is to provide multiple processors, each with its own unit. The control for the central processing unit (CPU) controls the execution of instructions in the arithmetic/logic unit; the control unit for the I/O device controls I/O transfers. By providing separate control units, a computer is created that can have several enabled control points at the same time and, thus, can carry on several activities simultaneously (1993:2-3).

Bernstein and Lewis further suggest that a program is sequential if during its execution no more than one control point can be enabled at a time (1993:12). And that a constructor is also sequential when only one enabled control point exists at a time (1993:19).

Thus, as Ragsdale points out, there are several very good reasons for trying to use existing sequential algorithms. They are as follows (1991:42):

(1)　You already understand the algorithms.

(2)　The algorithm's performance is well known.

(3)　Algorithms such as those in LINPACK are known to exhibit high accuracy with varied input data.

(4)　It is usually ill-advised to reinvent a solution when a satisfactory solution exists.

(2) A Sequential Model Using Seven Processors:

o　Group A farmers clear the fields, when they receive the high-yield coffee seeds
o　Group B farmers till the soil, when Group A farmers have finished
o　Group C farmers plant the seeds, when Group B farmers are finished
o　Group D farmers tend the coffee, when Group C farmers are finished
o　Group E farmers control for pests, when Group D farmers are finished
o　Group F farmers harvest the coffee, when Group E farmers are finished
o　Group G farmers load and deliver the coffee for sale to the government marketing board

Indeed, as Chandy and Misra (1988:4) observe, the notion of sequential control flow is evident in every aspect of computing. Turing Machines and von Neumann computers are examples of sequential devices. Flow charts and early programming languages were predicated on the sequential flow of control. Structured programming retained sequential control flow and called for problem decomposition based on the sequencing of tasks. Since many of the things we use daily, such as instructions for filling out forms and programming our video machines, are sequential, this may have influenced programming languages and the abstractions employed in program design. Thus, the prominence of sequential control flow is partly due to historical reasons, as early computing devices and programs were understood by simulating their executions sequentially.

(3) A Pipeline Using Seven Processors:

o Group A farmers clear the first field, leave it for Group B farmers and go to begin clearing the second field

o Group B farmers till the first field, leave it for Group C farmers and go to begin tilling the second Field

o Group C farmers plant the seeds in the first field, leave it for Group D farmers and go to begin planting seeds in the second field

o Group D farmers tend the coffee in the first field, leave it for Group E farmers and go on to begin tending the coffee in the second field

o Group E farmers control for pests in the first field, leave it for Group E farmers and go on to begin controlling for pests in the second field

o Group F farmers harvest the coffee in the first field, leave it for Group G farmers and go on the begin harvesting the coffee in the second field o Group G farmers load and deliver the coffee from the first field for sale to the government marketing board and waits for the coffee to be harvested in the second field

Indeed, this third model permits parallelism as every group can be working on different aspects of the farming process at the same time. The system requires a great deal of synchronization. If Group A farmers take a very long time to clear the fields, the groups will be waiting as follows:

o Group B farmers will be waiting for group A farmers to clear the fields in order to till the soil
o Group C farmers will be waiting for Group B farmers to till the soil in order to plant the seeds
o Group D farmers will be waiting for Group C farmers to plant the seeds in order to tend the coffee
o Group E farmers will be waiting for Group D farmers to tend to the coffee in order to control for pests
o Group F farmers will be waiting for Group E farmers to control for pests in order to harvest the coffee
o Group G farmers will be waiting for Group F farmers to harvest the coffee in order to load and deliver it for sale to the government marketing board.

According to Osterhaug, the pipeline technique is appropriate for applications in which the major functions are co-dependent and the data set or sets are very large. She notes that, for example, the technique would be appropriate for a signal-processing application that analyzes satellite data to determine a finite set of categories, assigns each data point to a category, assigns a color value to each data point, and then employs the results to create a colored image (1989:6-3).

Osterhaug also suggests the following algorithm for a pipeline application (1989:3):

(1) Create a set of processes, giving each one access to a set of shared data.

(2) Assign a task to each process.

(3) The first process performs calculations on a portion of the data, writes the results to shared memory, and notifies the next process that the results are available for processing.

(4) Add additional processes, giving the first process new data sets and having each subsequent process use the results of the previous process until all the work is done.

(5) When work runs out, each process terminates or, if there are other tasks to be done, relinquishes its processor or spins until it is assigned a new task.

(6) Proceed with serial execution.

Thus, as Wilkinson and Allen (1999:139) observe, in the pipeline technique, a problem is segmented into a series of tasks that have to be completed one after the other. In fact, these authors note, this is the basis of sequential programming. In pipelining, each task will be executed by a separate processor. Each pipeline process is called a pipeline *stage*. Each stage contributes to the overall problem and pass the information that is needed for subsequent stages. The authors also suggest that this parallelism can be looked at as a form of *functional decomposition*—i.e. a problem is divided into separate functions that must be performed, albeit in this case, the functions are performed in succession.

And for Chandy and Misra (1988:190), a pipelined network is a special kind of network because it consists of processes arranged in a linear fashion. In this case, data input at one end of a network are processed by the first process, which may then produce input for the next process in sequence, and so on.

In the case of *specialist parallelism*, for example, Carriero and Gelernter point out that programs are conceived in terms of a logical network. The need for such programs arises when an algorithm or a system to be modeled is best understood as a network in which each node executes a relatively autonomous computation, and inter-node communication follows predictable paths. The network may mirror a physical model or the logical structure of an algorithm (as in a pipelined or systolic computation). When there exists a physical system to be modeled, network-style solutions can be particularly transparent and natural. An example, is a circuit simulator that is modeled by a parallel program in which each circuit element is realized by a separate process (1990:19).

(4) A Message-passing System:

The description of the preceding pipeline solution can also serve as a description of a message-passing system, the farming procedures being the messages. A message-passing system will facilitate communication in the one direction to one processor of a pipeline.

A message-passing system will be required to handle the following additional requirements:

o   If a field is cleared, Group A farmers pass it directly to Group B farmers o If Group B farmers encounter a poorly cleared field, they give it back to Group A farmers

As Wilkinson and Allen point out, programming a message-passing multicomputer can be achieved by the following (1999:38):

(1) Designing a special parallel programming language;

(2) Extending the syntax/reserved words of an existing sequential high- level language to handle message passing; and

(3) Using an existing sequential high-level language and providing a library of external procedures for message passing.

Wilkinson and Allen add that, while there are examples of all three preceding approaches, perhaps the only common example of a special message-passing parallel programming language is the language referred to as *occam*, designed to be used with the message-passing processor named a *transputer*. In addition, these scholars note that examples of language extensions include CC+ (a small extension of C++) and Fortran M (a small extension to FORTRAN), both of which are used for parallel programming in general (1999:38-39).

Also, as Szymanski points out, another popular concept found in parallel algorithm is the use of message passing between some notion of *processes*. This is the kind of framework that can be found in parallel computing models such as Actors. He adds that a convenient programming idiom for expressing message passing algorithms in a functional language is the use of *shared list* to represent the stream of messages between two processes, and *functions* to represent the processes themselves (1991:180).

(5) The Use of Buffers:

With the preceding two systems, delay will be experienced because both processors must be willing to participate in a communication (e.g., Group B farmers must be willing to accept a cleared field from Group A farmers, and the Group A farmers must be willing to clear the field in good time and give it to Group B farmers). This problem can be avoided by the use of buffer in which messages can be stacked. This does not totally alleviate the problems because at times the buffer will be empty and at other times the buffer will be full.

According to Wilkinson and Allen (1999:58), in a buffered mode, send may start and return before the matching receive. Thus, it is imperative that specific buffer space be provided in an application.

And as Chandy and Misra (1988:175-176) observe, a message can be deposited in a channel provided there exists some empty buffer space in the channel to handle that message. In an *unbounded buffer model*, on the one hand, it is assumed that each channel has an unbounded amount of buffer space; hence, no sender is prevented from sending a message due to lack of buffer space. In a *bounded buffer model*, on the other hand, explicit bounds on the amount of buffer space for each channel are given. As such, a sender must wait to send if the buffer is full. In both cases, a receiver can receive a message only if the channel has one; a message is removed from the channel once it has been received. Moreover, in both cases, it is assumed that channels are error free and first-in-first-out (FIFO).

Also, as Bernstein and Lewis point out, most implementations of message passing employ buffers to temporarily store messages between the time they are sent and the time they are received. When infinite buffer space is available, an unbound number of messages can be stored for as long as necessary. However, real systems have only finite size buffers; thus, a sender may discover that the buffer is full. In which case, the message must be delayed until buffer space is freed or the system returns to "buffer full" exception (1993:205).

(6) Shared Memory:

With the buffers described in the preceding subsection, it is assumed that it is private to the two groups communicating. However, there is the possibility of the existent of a shared memory. This could be seen as a large buffer on which all of the farming tasks can be stacked. Care will obviously have to be exercised to make sure that there is no attempt to skip a task. At the other extreme, there is private space that belongs to just one farming group and no other group can access it without specific permission; for instance, clearing the fields may be seen as the private domain of the expert field clearers. This can be combined with the shared-space concept—i.e. a task can be accessible to only one group of farmers, but other tasks can be accessed by many groups of farmers.

As Wilkinson and Allen suggest, a natural way to extend the single processor model is to have multiple processors connected to multiple memory modules in a way that each processor can access memory module in a so-called *shared memory* configuration. The connection between the processors and the memory is through some *interconnection network*. A shared memory multiprocessor system uses a *single address space*, meaning that each location in the whole main memory system possesses a unique address and this address is used by each processor to access that location (1999:6).

Wilkinson and Allen further point out that most single processor systems incorporate the concept of *virtual memory*—i.e. a memory devised to hide the fact that the memory in real systems is hierarchical and it gives the illusion that one high-speed main memory exists in the system. It does this by automatically moving the contents of the main memory locations to and from the secondary disk memory. This is made possible by utilizing two addresses for each memory location: a *virtual address* (generated by the processor) and a *real address* (used to access the actual memory location. An automatic translation takes place between the virtual address and the real address employing a hardware look-up table referred to as a translation look-aside buffer (TLB). Virtual memory can be extended to a shared memory multiprocessor. However, each memory location will still have a unique read address, albeit processors could employ different virtual addresses to reference it (1999:6).

Programming a shared memory multiprocessor, Wilkinson and Allen also mention, involves having executable code stored in the memory for each processor to execute. The data for each program must also be stored in the shared memory; thus, each program could access all the data when it needs them. A programmer can employ different approaches to create an executable code and shared data for the processors. One approach is to design a new parallel language equipped with special parallel programming constructs and statements that facilitate the declaration of shared variables and parallel code sections. Then the compiler has the task of producing the final executable code from the programmer's specification. Another approach is to base parallel programming languages upon existing sequential programming languages such as FORTRAN and C/C++. An alternative approach is to use so-called *threads* that contain regular high- level language code sequences for individual processors. These code sequences can then access shared locations. However, as Wilkinson and Allen further note, from a programmer's perspective, the shared memory multiprocessor approach is attractive because of the convenience of sharing data (1999:6-7).

(7) A Processor Array:

One can presuppose that the farming community has a large number of farmers who are mentally challenged, each with her/his own farming task.

Then each of these could help to quickly complete a farming task. But because of their mental disability, they will have to be closely supervised. A supervisor will direct their every move. If at any point the supervisor decides that s/he does not require all of these helpers to work, s/he can direct them to ignore the next set of instructions. This will be useful if there are, say, only a few tasks, which will require particular skills, then the excess helpers can remain idle rather than trying to perform the task in an unsatisfactory manner.

For Chandy and Misra, a heuristic for processor array is to separate the concerns of computation and communication. A program is derived in two steps: the first deals with computation, and the second deals with communication. In the first step a synchronous parallel program is derived, ignoring issues dealing with network typology. The program defines a set of values to be computed—i.e. the values taken on by the variables of the program. In the second step, a network onto which the computation can be mapped efficiently is proposed. It is useful to segment the second step into two parts. First, the vertices at which each value is computed and which vertices need which values must be identified. At this stage, paths from vertices computing the values to vertices needing them are to be prescribed. In the second part, times—i.e. step numbers at which a value is computed at a vertex—must be proposed. This is to minimize memory requirements at each vertex. As Chandy and Misra also point out, timing to optimize memory requirements is often the most difficult part in deriving a solution for a synchronous array, and determining the computation at each vertex is usually trivial (1988:114).

(8) An Object-oriented Approach:

Instead of thinking about processors (people), it is possible to consider the objects (e.g., tasks). Consider one class of objects in detail: tilling the soil. There are many states a tilled soil can be in (e.g., deeply tilled for yam, shallow tilled for corn, medium tilled for rice, etc.). A Group C farmer who plants the coffee seeds will be interested in the state of the tilled soil; s/he may not be concerned about the operations that transformed the soil's state. The operations on the object are defined internally to the object. Thus, the operations of the state of tilled soil will be carried out by Group B farmers who are responsible for tilling, albeit the issue of scheduling the procedure is independent of this approach. Consequently, each class of object (i.e. farming task) will have its own operations clearly defined.

"Over the past few years," asserts Booch, "object-oriented (OO) technology has evolved in diverse segments of the computer science as a means of managing the complexity inherent in many different kinds of systems. The object model has proven to be a very powerful and unifying concept" (1994:v). It is this characteristic of OO Programming (OOP) that will make it quite suitable for employing it in insuring development project accountability in African countries. Indeed, it is this characteristic that has made it possible for the OO paradigm to be used throughout the world for such diverse domains as the administration of banking transactions, the automation of bowling alleys, the management of public utilities, the mapping of the human genome, and for writing new generation operating systems such as avionics systems, database systems, multimedia applications, telephony systems, etc. many such projects employ OO technology because there seems to be no other way to economically produce a lasting and resilient programming system.

A major aspect of OOP is that programming in OO language is more than just learning new functions, syntax, etc. For instance, when a person studies COBOL, another procedural language, s/he could simply apply the knowledge gained from learning Modula-2 to COBOL. This cannot be done with OO languages, because they require a new way of thinking about decomposition. The person is forced to think not in terms of data structures, but in terms of objects—i.e. a bundle of variables and related methods, or also referred to as "abstract data types." In essence, the differences hinge upon the fact that, while structured design methods build upon structured programming, OO design builds upon OO programming.

The undergirding notion of an object is that of simulation. While most programs are written with very little reference to the real world objects with which they are designed to work, in OO methodology a program should be written to simulate the states and activities of real world objects. This calls for a programmer to not only look at data structures when modeling an object, but to also look at methods associated with that object— i.e. functions that modify the object's attributes.

(9) A Functional Model:

A single function can be defined that will model the entire farming process. The function is applied to the farming tasks and the result is money received by selling the harvest to the government marketing board. This can be decomposed into a number of smaller functions, many of which will be similar to the message-passing model described earlier. For example, the role of the field clearing farmers (Group A) can be seen as a function that takes a stream of bushy plots of lands, cuts down the bushes, and produces fields that are ready for tilling.

Thus, as Williams (1990:7) points out, functional models are often based on lazy evaluation—i.e. only those values that are needed are evaluated. Consequently, lazy evaluations do not lead to parallelism.

In essence, "there is more to functional programming than simply programming in a functional language," as MacLennan correctly asserts. With this in mind, he characterizes *functional programming*, also referred to as *applicative programming* and *value-oriented programming*, as comparable in importance to structured programming. Thus, he argues, functional programming has values as a discipline of thought even in the absence of functional programming languages (1999:iii, 3).

Functional programming can be treated as a means for reliably deriving programs and as a technique for analyzing programs and proving that they are correct. It can be employed this way, even if the eventual implementation language is a conventionally imperative one. In this way, the value of functional programming languages is naturally illustrated. And by emphasizing methodology rather than specific languages, functional programming becomes quite useful in software engineering, software prototyping, formal specification, language systems (i.e. compilers and environments), data structure, and algorithm analysis (MacLennan 1990:iii- 1v).

Most extant functional languages are experimental in nature—i.e. they are undergoing an evolutionary process, which also suggests that the popular languages of today may be obsolete tomorrow. One exception to this phenomenon is LISP, a quasi-functional language (MacLennan 1990:v). Having been around for 40 years, LISP will likely be around for a quite a few more.

Functional programming has six major advantages that make it pliant for developing computer programs that can address shortcomings in accountability of development projects in African countries. These major advantages, according to MacLennan (1990:3-5), are summarized as follows:

(1) It dispenses with ubiquitous assignment operation.

(2) It encourages thinking at *higher levels of abstraction* by providing mechanisms (higher-order functions) for modifying the behavior of existing programs and combining existing programs.

(3) It provides a paradigm for programming *massively parallel computers*—i.e. computers with hundreds of thousands, perhaps millions of processors.

(4) It is applicable in artificial intelligence (AI).

(5) It is valuable in developing *executable specification* and *prototype implementations.*

(6) Its is connected to computer theory by providing a framework for viewing many of the decidability questions of programming and computers, a simpler framework than that provided by the usual approaches.

In essence, functional programming can be very useful for developing computer programs that would insure accountability of development projects in African countries because of two considerations. The first is the role of mathematics—a principal tool for symbolic manipulation. The second is the advantages of the use of functions, stemming from the fact that applicative (pure) expressions are *referentially unambiguous*—i.e., they possess a unique *referent.*

Conclusion

Evident from the preceding discussion is that to develop a parallel program for insuring development project accountability in African countries requires the development of methods that will support the development of parallel software for one or more parallel architectures. The good news is that the possibility of methods for parallel programming is currently under investigation for limited domains. However, these domains need to be expanded to include all problems and target architectures. Also needed are tools to support the design and development of parallel solutions. The ones that currently exist are not general purpose or sufficient to cover all needs.

An alternative approach will be to investigate the likelihood of defining an ideal machine that is mappable onto all real parallel hardwares. A more realistic goal may be to define a maximum machine that entails all different models of parallelism. A great deal of work lies ahead in order to bring either one of these approaches to fruition.

Chapter 5

Concurrent Programming

Since a concurrent program can specify two or more processes that cooperate in performing a task, it can be used to insure accountability in development projects in African countries. This is because each process is a sequential program that executes a sequence of statements. Processes cooperate by communicating, and they communicate by using shared variables of message passing. The use of shared variables enables one process to write into a variable that is read by another. And the use of message passing allows one process to send a message that is received by the other. Consequently, concurrent programs are inherently more complex than sequential programs (Andrews 1991:1).

Nonetheless, computer scientists have been able to construct large concurrent programs as hierarchies of smaller components. Each of these components is given a well-defined function that can be implemented and tested as an almost independent program. The components and their combinations are given reproducible behavior, and the verification and testing of such programs take place much faster than they will change due to new requirements (for details, see Axford 1989, Bernstein and Lewis 1993, Burns 1988, Dahmke 1986, Gehani and McGettrick 1988, Goldberg 1984, Hansen 1978, Hansen 1977, Hartman 1977, Hunt 1997, Kaehler and Petterson 1986, Magee and Kramer 1999, Reppy 1999, Schneider 1997, Smith 1995, Wexler 1989, Whiddett 1987, and Winston 1998).

Thus, concurrent programming has emerged as one of the most important computer techniques in recent years because multiprocessors, particularly of microcomputers, have become attractive alternatives to traditional maxicomputers. According to Gehani and McGettrick (1988:v), the reasons for concurrent programming's emergence include:

(a) Notational convenience and conceptual elegance in writing systems in which many events occur concurrently, for example, in operating systems, real-time systems and database systems.

(b) Preserving the structure of concurrent algorithms.

(c) Speeding up program execution on genuine multiprocessing hardware such as a network of microcomputers.

(d) Speeding up program execution even on uniprocessors; concurrent programming allows lengthy input/output operations and the CPU operation to proceed in parallel.

Formal tools for concurrent programs hinge on assertional reasoning. A program state is characterized by a predicate referred to as an assertion, and the effects of executing program statements are characterized by predicate transformers. The basis for a systematic method for delineating programs that satisfy specified properties is the assertional reasoning, which also facilitates insight into tradeoffs between different language notations. Different language mechanisms have been suggested for specifying concurrent execution, communication, and synchronization. The most important mechanisms are semaphores, monitors, those based on message passing, and survey programming languages that use different combinations. Important paradigms that have been offered for concurrent programming include solution strategies and programming approaches that can be used for a wide variety of problems. Most concurrent programs are derived from putting together a small number of simple structures that can be viewed as instances of a few standard problems (Andrews 1991:1-2).

A program property is an attribute that is true of every possible history of that program, thus of all executions of the program. Properties can be formulated in terms of two special kinds of properties: (1) *safety* property which asserts that the program never enters a bad state, i.e. one in which some variables have undesirable effects; (2) *liveness* property which asserts that a program eventually enters a good state, i.e. one in which the variables all have desirable values (Andrews 1991:4).

An example of a safety property is *partial correctness* which asserts that if a program terminates, the final state is correct; i.e. the right result has been computed. If the program fails to terminate, it may never produce the correct answer, albeit no history exists where the program has terminated without yielding the correct answer. An example of a liveness property is *termination* which asserts that a program will eventually terminate; i.e. every history of a program is finite. A property that combines partial correctness and termination is *total correctness* which asserts that a program always terminates with a correct answer (Andrews 1991:4).

Another example of a safety property is *mutual exclusion* which asserts that at most one process at a time is executing in its critical section. The bad state in this case would be one in which actions in critical sections in different processes are both eligible for execution. Another example of a safety property is *absence of deadlock* for which a bad state is one in which all processes are blocked, i.e. there are no eligible actions. Finally, another example of a liveness property is *eventual entry to a critical section* for which the good state for each process is one in which its critical section is eligible (Andrews 1991:5).

Given a program and a desired property, there are three ways one can demonstrate that the program satisfies a desired property. The first technique is *testing* or *debugging*, which can be characterized as "kick the program and see what happens." This is akin to enumerating some of the possible histories of a program and verifying that they are acceptable. The second technique is *operational reasoning*, which can be characterized as "exhaustive case analysis." In this technique, all possible execution histories of a program are enumerated by considering all the ways operations of each process might be interleaved. Unfortunately, the number of histories in a concurrent program is generally enormous, making the approach cumbersome. The third technique is *assertional reasoning*, which can be characterized as "abstract analysis." In this approach, formulae of predicate logic referred to as *assertions* are employed to characterize sets of states— e.g., all states in which x > 0 (Andrews 1991:5).

However, as Andrews points out, one must be wary of testing alone, since it can only reveal the presence of errors, not their absence. Moreover, he adds, concurrent programs are extremely difficult to test and debug since it is difficult to stop all processes at once in order to examine their state, and each execution of the same program may produce a different history because actions might be interleaved in a different order (Andrews 1991:5- 6).

Sequential programs with tools for specifying concurrency, communication, and synchronization can be extended by concurrent programs.

Unfortunately, properties of concurrent programs cannot have a sound and complete axiomatization as a logical system. This is because program behavior has to include arithmetic and Gödel's incompleteness theorem—a well known result in logic which states that no formal logical system that axiomatizes arithmetic can be complete. However, a logic that extends another logic can be *relatively complete*, i.e. that it introduces no source of incompleteness beyond that already in the logic it extends (Andrews 1991:7, 16). Fortunately, relative completeness is good enough for evaluating development projects since the arithmetic properties that are employed for such an exercise are certainly true, even if not all of them can be proved formally.

Another major problem that can arise in concurrent programs is interference, which occurs when one process takes an action that invalidates assumptions made by another process. There are four ways for avoiding interference. First, if the *write set* (the set of variables that it assigns to a process) of one process is *disjoint* from the reference set of a second, and vice versa, then the two processes cannot interfere. Second, make a *weaker* assertion about shared variables that could be made if a process were executed in isolation. Third, employ a *global invariant* to capture the relation between shared variables. Finally, use *synchronization* to ignore an assignment statement that is within angle brackets when considering non-interference obligations (Andrews 1991:57-75).

Thus, in order to appreciate the usefulness of the concurrent programming approach, the following sections focus on concurrent design principles, types of concurrent programs, concurrent programming languages, and an example of a simplified concurrent program for a government banking system in Africa. In the end, a conclusion is offered based on the discussion.

Concurrent Design Principles

There is consensus within the literature on concurrent programming that the design principles of a good concurrent program must include the following interrelated qualities: simplicity, reliability, adaptability, efficiency, and portability. A close look at each of these program qualities and how they can be achieved follows.

Simplicity. Since written concurrent programs are so large that one cannot understand them all at once, a programmer must reason about them in smaller pieces. Each piece must be written so small that it should be trivial to understand in itself. The ideal piece should be no more than a page of text, so that one can understand it at a glance (Hansen 1977:4, Gehani and McGettrick 1988:142, Bernstein and Lewis 1993:18).

The program could be studied page by page as one reads a book. In the end, however, when one had understood what all the pieces do, s/he must still be able to see what their combined effects as a whole will be. It the program comprises many pages, this can only be done by ignoring most the detailed knowledge about the pieces and relying on a much simpler description of what they do and how they work together (Hansen 1977:4).

The program pieces must make it possible to perform well-defined, simple functions. Program pieces will then be combined into larger configurations to carry out more complicated functions. This design method is effective in that it splits a complicated task into simpler ones. First, one must convince her/himself that the pieces work individually, and then s/he can think about how they work together. Second, it is essential that one is able to forget how a piece works in detail—otherwise, the problem becomes too cumbersome. In doing so, however, one makes the fundamental assumption that the piece always will do the same when it carries out its function. Otherwise, one cannot afford to ignore the detailed behavior of that piece in her/his reasoning about the entire system (Hansen 1977:4-5).

Thus, reproducible behavior is imperative in building program pieces that one wishes to create and study in small steps. One must clearly keep this in mind when s/he selects the kind of program pieces that can be used to create large concurrent programs. One often takes for granted the ability to repeat program behavior when s/he writes sequential programs. In this case, the sequence of events is completely defined by the program and its input data. However, in a concurrent program, simultaneous events take place at rates not fully controlled by the programmer. They hinge upon the presence of other jobs in the machine and the scheduling policy used to execute them. Thus, a conscious effort must be made to design concurrent programs with reproducible behavior (Hansen 1977:5).

The idea of reasoning first about what a piece does and then studying how it does it in detail is most effective, if a programmer can repeat this process by explaining each piece in terms of simpler pieces which themselves are built from still simpler pieces. So, many concurrent programmers confine themselves to hierarchical structures composed of layers of program pieces. By each part only depending on a small number of other parts, the process will be simplified, thereby increasing a programmer's understanding of hierarchical structures. S/he will then try to build structures that have minimal interfaces between their parts. This is a challenging task in machine language, since the slightest programming mistake can make an instruction destroy any instruction or variable. Programs written in abstract languages (e.g., Fortran, Algol, and Pascal) are incapable of modifying themselves. Nonetheless, they still have broad interfaces in the form of global variables that can be changed by every statement, intentionally or mistakenly. Thus, Concurrent Pascal, which makes it possible to divide the global variables into smaller parts, is frequently used for concurrent programming. Each of these parts is accessible to only a small number of statements (Hansen 1977:5).

In essence, the major contribution of a good programming language to simplicity is to provide an abstract readable notation that makes the parts and structure of programs obvious to a reader. An abstract program language can suppress machine detail such as addresses, registers, bit patterns, interrupts, and sometimes even the number of available processors. The language relies, therefore, on abstract concepts such as variables, data types, synchronizing operations, and concurrent processes. This yields program texts that are often an order of magnitude shorter than those written in machine language. The textual reduction, in turn, considerably simplifies program engineering (Hansen 1977:5-6).

Reliability. Even the most readable language notation does not prevent a programmer from making mistakes. In looking for these in large programs, one needs all the assistance s/he can get. The following techniques can be profitable (Hansen 1977:6):

(1) correctness proofs
(2) proofreading
(3) compilation checks
(4) execution checks
(5) systematic testing

Among the useful verification approaches, those that reveal errors at the earliest possible time during the program development must be emphasized to achieve reliability as early as possible. Concurrent Pascal pushes the role of compilation checks to the limit and reduces the use of execution checks as much as possible. Extensive compilation checks are possible only with redundant language notation. The programmer must specify important properties in at least two different ways, so that the compiler can look for possible inconsistencies. One way is to use declarations to introduce variables and their types before they are employed in statements. The compiler could then easily derive this information from the statements, as long as these statements were always correct (Hansen 1977:6-7, Axford 1989:177-188). And with a reliable channel, every message sent eventually becomes eligible to be received (Schneider 1997:378).

Adaptability. Since the development of a large program is quite expensive, it makes sense that it be built to last for several years. As time passes and a user's needs change, the program must also be modified to meet those needs. Quite often, the modifications are done by people who did not develop the program in the first place. Their main difficulty will be to find out how the program works and whether it will still work after the changes have been made (Hansen 1977:8).

An interesting relationship exists between programming errors and changing user requirements. They are both sources of instability in the program construction process that makes it difficult to reach a state in which a programmer has complete confidence in what a program does. They are the result of programmers' inability to fully comprehend the entire details of a large program. The relative frequencies of program errors and changing requirements are critical. If programming introduces numerous errors that are difficult to locate, many of them may still be in the program when changes of its functions are requested by users. An unstable product is the end result when a programmer constantly finds her/himself changing a system that s/he never succeeded in making work correctly initially. Conversely, when program errors are located and corrected at a much faster rate than the system develops, then the addition of a new component (or a change) to the program can lead to a stable situation in which the current version of the program works reliably and predictably (Hansen 1977:8).

Since a hierarchical structure consists of program pieces that can be studied one at a time, it makes it easier to read the program and get an initial understanding of what it does and how it does it. Once a programmer has that insight, the consequences of changing a hierarchical program become very clear to her/him. When s/he changes a part of a program pyramid, s/he must be prepared to inspect and perhaps change the program parts that are on top of it, for they are the only ones upon which s/he can possibly depend (Hansen 1977:8-9).

Portability. For economic reasons, it is desirable to be able to use the same program on a variety of computers. Many users possess different computers; they sometimes replace them with new ones; and they quite often would like to share programs developed on different machines. Thus, portability is only practical when programs are written in abstract languages that mask the differences between computers as much as possible. Otherwise, extensive rewriting and testing will be required to move programs from one machine to another. Program portability can be achieved in the following ways (Hansen 1977:9):

(1) by having *different compilers* for different machines. This is only practical for the most widespread languages.

(2) by having a *single compiler* that can be modified to generate code for different machines. This requires a clear separation within the compiler of those parts that check programs and those that generate code.

(3) by having a *single computer* that can be simulated efficiently on different machines.

Thus, for the design of a language for which portability is a major issue, the applicability to a wide variety of architectures must be a fundamental concern (Gehani and McGettrick 1988:142).

Efficiency. Program efficiency is critical for saving time for people waiting for results and for reducing computation costs. Concurrent programs owe their efficiency on the following features (Hansen 1977:9, Bernstein and Lewis 1993:188):

(1) special-purpose algorithms
(2) static store allocation
(3) minimal run-time checking

Dynamic store algorithms that move programs and data segments around during execution can be grossly inefficient that a programmer cannot control. Concurrent Pascal does not require garbage collection or demand paging of storage. Instead, it employs static allocation of store among a fixed number of processes. And the compiler determines the store requirements. When programs are written in assembly language, one cannot predict what they will do. Most computers rely upon hardware mechanisms to prevent such programs from destroying one another. In Concurrent Pascal, however, most of this protection is guaranteed by the compiler and is not supported by hardware mechanisms during execution. This drastic reduction of run-time checking is made possible because all of the programs are written in an abstract language (Hansen 1977:10, Magee and Kramer 1999:262). And as Gehani and McGettrick (1988:142) point out, it is the concern for simplicity that reinforces the need for efficiency.

In sum, to achieve simplicity and reliability, a concurrence programmer will have to depend exclusively upon a machine-independent language that makes programs readable and extensive compilation checks possible. To achieve adaptability, efficiency and portability, a programmer must employ the simplest possible store allocation.

Types of Concurrent Programs

Concurrent programs can be classified into three categories: (1) the Solo operating system, (2) the Job Stream system, and (3) the Real-Time Scheduler. A discussion of these program types follows.

Solo Operating System. First written in the Concurrent Pascal language, a Solo operating system is a simple, but useful, operating system used to develop and distribute Pascal programs. This system supports editing, compilation, and storage of Sequential and Concurrent Pascal programs. These programs can access either console, cards, printer, tape or disk (the first two hardly used these days) at several levels—character by character, page by page, file by file, or by direct device access. Concurrent processes handle input, processing, and output files. Pascal programs can call one another recursively and pass arbitrary parameters among themselves (Hansen 1977:69).

According to Hansen, to the system programmer, a Solo operating system is quite different from many other operating for the following reasons (1977:69-70):

(1) Less than 4 percent of it is written in machine language. The rest is written in Sequential and Concurrent Pascal.

(2) In contrast to machine-oriented languages, Pascal does not contain low-level programming features, such as registers, addresses, and interrupts. These are all handled by the virtual machine which executes compiled programs.

(3) System protection is achieved largely by means of compile-time checking of access rights. Run-time checking is minimal and is not supported by hardware mechanisms.

(4)   Solo is the first major example of a hierarchical concurrent program implemented by means of abstract data types (classes, monitors, and processes).

(5)   The complete system consisting of more than 100,000 machine
words of code (including two compilers) was developed by a student and [Hansen] in less than a year.

Thus, to appreciate the usefulness of Concurrent Pascal, suggests Hansen,
a programmer needs a good understanding of at least one operating system such as Solo that is written in the language (Hansen 1977:70).

Job Stream System. This operating system compiles and executes a stream
of user programs input from a computer and output on a line printer.
Concurrent Pascal is used to write a job stream, and Sequential Pascal is
employed to write user programs. The system provides informal access
and fast response to short jobs (Hansen 1977:149).

A job stream system uses the disk to store its own system programs and
the temporary data to user jobs. A job stream system considers itself the
owner of the disk, since users cannot store programs and data perma-
nently on the disk. Thus, a job stream can use the file system developed
for a Solo operating system (Hansen 1977:153).

Real-Time Scheduler. This operating system is used for process control
applications in which a fixed number of concurrent tasks are implemented
periodically with frequencies chosen by a human operator (Hansen
1977:189). It is a system in which timing requirements are an essential
part of its specification (Axford 1989:2).

According to Axford (1989:2), "timing requirements" include things such as the maximum allowable time delay between a specified input and the action of the responding output. The most common type of timing requirement, he notes, is an upper limit on a response time. He further adds that, in many cases, the response time is not specified very accurately.

Axford provides the following examples of Real-Time systems (1989:2-3):

Operating Systems—One of the main functions of a computer operating system is to handle input and output to peripheral devices (e.g., to access files on disc). Now, peripheral devices operate at speeds that are tightly constrained by their mechanical construction or by standardised interface protocols. If the operating system is to perform efficiently (or sometimes even to work at all), it must service each peripheral device more-or-less at the speed of that device. For example, it must be prepared to read a block from disc when the read head is positioned over the required block. If the operating system is too slow, the block will pass by and it will not be available again until the disc has done a complete revolution and the block is back under the read head once more. The time for the disc to do a complete revolution is quite long in computing terms!

Furthermore, operating systems are usually required to operate many different devices at once. This imposes quite severe and complex real-time requirements upon the system.

Transaction Processing Systems—These include point-of-sale (POS) systems such as those used in supermarkets with laser bar-code readers at the checkouts; automatic tellers in banks; ticket booking systems for airlines, theatres, etc. Such systems must have response times of a few seconds at most, or customers can become impatient and business may be lost as a result.

Industrial Process Control—Included here is the computer control of all sorts of industrial processes: whether it be a car production line, an oil refinery, a chemical plant or simply a specialised piece of machinery. Such computer systems are used not only to determine the sequencing and timing of complicated series of operations, but also to gather and process performance data, for quality monitoring and control, for detecting and rectifying exceptional conditions (such as a machine jamming), and many other purposes. Real-time requirements are common in these systems.

Embedded Systems—The term *embedded system* refers to any computer system which is built into a larger piece of equipment and functions as a component of it. Embedded systems are becoming extremely common: in the home, from burglar alarms to compact disc players and central heating systems; elsewhere, from military weapons systems to photocopiers, and from fly-by-wire aircraft to printing presses. Again, all these systems have real-time aspects to them.

Communications—E.g. System X telephone exchanges, data communications networks, cellular car telephone systems, satellite communications, military communications, local area computer networks, local area networks for distributed computer control of factories, ships, aircraft, etc. The great majority of modern communication systems rely heavily on computers and the software is typically required to meet stringent real-time requirements.

In essence, a Real-Time system forces a programmer to specify and subsequently guarantee an upper bound to execution time.

Concurrent Programming Languages

There now exist many languages that support concurrent programming. Little can be gained in looking at all languages with concurrent programming facilities. Nonetheless, it makes sense to briefly describe each of the following languages which form a representative subset based on both the shared memory and the message passing models.

Concurrent Pascal is a programming language for structured programming of computer operating systems. It extends the sequential programming language Pascal with concurrent programming tools referred to as processes, monitors (Gehani and McGettrick 1988:73) and classes (Hartman 1977:1).

Modula-2 evolved from an earlier language called Modula, which itself was based on Pascal. The main features of Modula-2, which are missing in Pascal, are: (a) a program structuring facility known as a *module*, and (b) facilities for concurrent programming (Axford 1989:123).

MOD is a language for distributed programming. As such, it is a high-level language system which attempts to address high communications costs and the inability to use shared variables and procedures for inter-processor synchronization and communication. It does so by creating an environment conducive to efficient and reliable network software construction (Gehani and McGettrick 1988:93).

Concurrent C is an extension of the C program, so that it can be used to write concurrent programs that can run efficiently on both single computers and multicomputers. The concurrent programming extensions to C are based on the *rendezvous* concept—that is, the extensions include mechanisms for the declaration and creation of processes, for process synchronization and interaction, and for process termination and abortion (Gehani and McGettrick 1988:112).

Ada is intended for the use in both conventional programming and real-time embedded systems and for distributed processing. Consequently, Ada includes concurrency mechanisms as a fundamental aspect of the language. It aims to be reasonably efficient when implemented on distributed systems (without shared memory) as well as on uniprocessors and multiprocessors (with shared memory). Ada, therefore, uses a synchronous message passing mechanism based on the *rendezvous* concept discussed earlier. Processes in the language are referred to as *tasks* that depend upon the particular implementation employed. Each task is defined by a special syntax (Axford 1989:135).

Concurrent PC DOS is the first in a series of new operating systems for the IBM Personal Computer and IBM-compatible computers. The language combines many features of previous operating systems into a more-or-less unified whole. It can support concurrency and windows, and comes with a number of useful utilities such as a word processor and a communication program. Also, it can support up to three users (Dahmke 1986:1, 5).

Concurrent ML is an extension of Standard ML (SML) with independent processes and higher-order communication and synchronization primitives. Its power hinges on the fact that a wide range of communication and synchronization abstractions can be programmed using a small collection of primitives. The communication and synchronization operations are first- class values, in much the same way that functions are first-class values in higher-order languages (Reppy 1999:ix).

Occam is an abstract programming language whose development has been closely associated with that of the transputer—a programmable VLSI device containing communication links for point-to-point inter-transputer connections. Occam's concurrency model has been greatly influenced by the need to provide the same programming techniques on a single transputer and a network of transputers. The transputer's effect on the design of Occam is negligible compared with Occam's influence over the hardware development (Burns 1988:3, Wexler 1989:9).

In sum, unlike sequential programming languages, no consensus seems to have emerged in terms of the right facilities for concurrent programming. This leaves unanswered many important questions about the design of concurrent programming languages.

An Example of a Simplified Concurrent Program for a Government Banking System in Africa

To illustrate the preceding techniques, consider the following example of a simplified government banking system in Africa. Suppose a government bank has a collection of accounts, allows government rice dealers to transfer money from one account to another, and has a government auditor to check for embezzlement. Let the accounts be represented by *account*[1:*n*]. A transaction that transfers $5,000 from an account *x* to account *y* could then be implemented by the *Transfer* process in Figure 1. In that process, we assume that *x* *y*, that there are sufficient funds, and that both accounts are valid (i.e. both x and y are between 1 and *n*). In the assertions in *Transfer*, X and Y are logical variables.

```
var account[1:n]: int
Transfer::        { account[x] = X , account[y] = Y
                  { account[x] : = account[x] - 5000
                  account[y] : = account[y] + 5000
```

$$account[x] = \text{X-5000} \ , \ account[y] = \text{Y+5000}$$

Auditor::   **var** *total* := 0, i : = 1, *embezzle* := false

$\{total = account[1] + ... + account[i\text{-}1]\}$

do i # n 6 $\{C1: total = account[1] + ... + account[i - 1]$
, i # n $\}$

          Total := *total* + *account*[i]; i := i + 1
          $\{C2: total = account[1] + ... + account[i - 1]\}$

od

$\{(total = account[1] + ... + account[n]) \ , i = n\}$

If *total*   CASH 6 *embezzle* := true **fi**

Figure 1: Government bank transfer and auditing problem

Let CASH be the total amount of cash in all accounts. The *Auditor* process in Figure 1 checks for embezzlement by iterating through the accounts, summing the amount in each, then comparing the total to CASH.

As programmed in Figure 1, *Transfer* executes as a single atomic action, so the *Auditor* will not see a state in which *account*[*x*] has been debited and then finish the audit without seeing the (pending) credit into *account*[*y*]. However, this is not sufficient to prevent interference. The problem is that, if *Transfer* executes while index *i* in *Auditor* is between *x* and *y*, the old amount in one of the accounts will already have been added to *total*, and later the new amount in the other account will be added, leading the *Auditor* incorrectly to believe funds have been embezzled. More precisely, the assignments in *Transfer* interfere with *Auditor* assertions *C1* and *C2*.

To avoid interference between the processes in Figure 1, additional synchronization is needed. One approach is to employ mutual exclusion to hide critical assertions *C1* and *C2*. This is achieved by placing the entire **do** loop in *Auditor* within angle brackets and, thus, making it atomic. Unfortunately, this has the effect of making almost all of *Auditor* execute without interruption. An alternative approach is to use condition synchronization to keep *Transfer* from executing if doing so will interfere with *C1* and *C2*. In particular, one can replace the unconditional atomic action in *Transfer* by the following conditional atomic action:

{ **await** $(x$ **and** $y < i)$ **or** $(x >$ **and** $y > i)$ 6
$\qquad account[x] := account[x] - 5000; account[y] := account[y] + 5000$ }

This second approach has the effect of making *Transfer* delay only when *Auditor* is at a critical point between accounts x and y.

As the preceding government banking example illustrates, mutual exclusion and condition synchronization can *always* be used to avoid interference. They are often required because the other techniques by themselves are often insufficient.

In most African countries, customer complaints about unfair treatment by government establishments abound. Some government establishments, such as hospitals and rice stores, use the following method to ensure that customers are serviced in order of arrival. Upon entering the establishment, the customer draws a number that is one larger than the number held by any other customer. The customer the waits until all customers holding smaller numbers have been serviced. This algorithm is implemented by a number dispenser and by a display indicating which customer is being served. If the establishment has one employee behind the service counter, customers are served one at a time in their order of arrival. This idea can be used to implement a fair critical section protocol.

Let *number* and *next* be integers that are initially 1, and let $turn[1:n]$ be an array of integers, each of which is initially 0. To enter its critical section, process $P[i]$ first sets $turn[i]$ to the current value of *number* and then increments *number*. These comprise a single atomic action to make sure that customers draw unique numbers. Process $P[i]$ then waits until the value of *next* is equal to the number it drew. In particular, the following predicate must be a variant (Andrews 1991:112-3):

{*Ticket*: (*P*[*i*] is in its critical section) | (*turn*[*i*] = *next*)
(i,j: 1 # i,j # n, i   j: *turn*[*i*] = 0 " *turn*[*i*]   *turn*[*j*])}

The second conjunct states that non-zero values of *turn* are unique; therefore, at most *turn*[*i*] is equal to next. When its critical section is completed, *P*[*i*] increments *next*, again as an atomic action.

This protocol yields the algorithm that appears in Figure 2. Predicate *Ticket* is a global invariant since *number* is read and incremented as an atomic action and *next* is incremented as an atomic action. Thus, at most, one process can be in its critical section. Absence of deadlock and unnecessary delay also follow because non-zero values in *turn* are unique. Moreover, if scheduling is weakly fair, the algorithm ensures eventual entry since once a delay condition becomes true, it remains so (Andrews 1991:113).

---

var *number* := 1, *next* := 1, *turn*[1:*n*] : **int** := ([*n*] 0)
{ *TICKET*: (*P*[*i*] is in its critical section) | (*turn*[*i*] = *next*)
(i,j: 1 # i,j # n, i   j: *turn*[*i*] = 0 w *turn*[*i*]   *turn*[*j*]) }
P[*i*: 1..*n*]:: **do** true v
                    ¢*turn*[*i*] := *number*; *number* := *number* + 1 ƒ
                    ¢**await** *turn*[*i*] = *next*ƒ
                    critical section
                    ¢*next* := *next* + 1ƒ
                    non-critical section
              od

Figure 2: The ticket algorithm: Coarse-grained solution

The ticket algorithm has one potential problem that is common in algorithms that use incrementing counters: i.e. the values of *number* and *next* are unbounded. When the ticket algorithms runs for a long time, incrementing a counter will eventually cause arithmetic overflow. However, this problem can be solved by resetting the counters to a small value, say one, any time they get too large. If the largest value is at least as large as *n*, then the values of turn[i] will be unique (Andrews 1991:113).

Since synchronization is basic to concurrent programs, it is desirable to have special tools to assist in designing and correcting synchronization protocols and that can be used in blocking processes that must be delayed. *Semaphores* are one of the first such tools and certainly one of the most vital (Andrews 1991:172). A semaphore is an instance of abstract data type that has a representation that is manipulated only by two special operations, **P** and **V**. The **V** operation signals the occurrence of an event, and the **P** operation is used to delay a process until an event has occurred. Specifically, the two operations must be implemented so that they pre-serve the following property for every semaphore in a program:

> **Semaphore Invariant.** For semaphore *s*, let *nP* be the number of com-pleted **P** operations, and let *nV* be the number of completed **V** opera-tions. If *init* is the initial value of *s*, then in all visible program states, *nP* # *nV* + *init* (Andrews 1991:172).

In essence, execution of a **P** operation potentially delays until an adequate number of **V** operations has been executed (Andrews 1991:172). Thus, semaphores make it easy to protect critical sections and can be used in a disciplined way to implement condition synchronization. They can also be implemented in more than one way. Particularly, they can be imple-mented using busy waiting, but they also have implementations that interact with a process scheduler to yield synchronization without busy waiting (Andrews 1991:171).

The concept of semaphore can be useful in synchronizing railroad traffic in African countries to avoid the frequent train collisions. A railroad semaphore in the form of a flag can indicate whether a track ahead is clear or is occupied by another train. As a train proceeds, semaphores can be set and cleared, with semaphores remaining set far enough behind the train so that another train has time to stop if necessary.

In addition, consider the general situation in which there are multiple producers and consumers of a product in an African country. The solution illustrates another use of semaphores as signaling flags. It also introduces the important concept of a split binary semaphore.

As Andrews (1991:182) points out, in the producers/consumers problem, producers send messages that are received by consumers. The processes communicate using a single shared buffer, which is manipulated by two operations: *deposit* and *fetch*. Producers insert messages into the buffer by calling *deposit*, and consumers receive messages by calling *fetch*. To make sure that messages are not overwritten before being received and are only received once, execution of *deposit* and *fetch* must alternate, with *deposit* executed first.

As with barrier synchronization, Andrews adds, the way to specify the required alternation property is to use incrementing counters to indicate when a process reaches critical execution points. The critical points here are starting and completing executions of *deposit* and *fetch*. Therefore, *inD* and *afterD* can be integers that count the number of times producers have started and finished executing *deposit*. Also, *inF* and *afterF* can be integers that count the number of times consumers have started and finished executing *fetch*. Then the predicate that specifies that *deposit* and *fetch* alternate is the following (Andrews 1991:182-3):

$$PC: inD \text{ \# } afterF + 1 \text{ , } inF \text{ \# } afterD$$

Put into words, the preceding predicate indicates that *deposit* can be started at most one more time than *fetch* has been completed and that *fetch* can be started no more times than *deposit* has been completed.

If messages are produced at approximately the same rate at which they are consumed, a single buffer can provide reasonable performance since the process would not generally have to wait very long to gain access to the buffer. However, since producer and consumer execution is "bursty," Andrews suggests that the *bounded buffer*—namely, the problem of implementing a multislot communication buffer—be used to solve the problem, since general semaphores can be used as resource counters (1991:185).

In this case, the buffer will contain a queue of messages that have been deposited but not yet fetched. This queue can be represented by a linked list or by an array. The buffer will be represented by *buf*[1:*n*], where *n* is greater than 1. Let *front* be the index of the message at the front of the queue, and let *rear* be the index of the first empty slot past the message at the rear of the queue. Initially, *front* and *rear* are set to the same value, say 0. Then the producer deposits messages *m* into the buffer be executing the following (Andrews 1991:186):

deposit: *buf*[*rear*] := *m*; *rear* := *rear* **mod** *n* + 1

And the consumer fetches a message into its local variable *m* by executing the following:

fetch: *m* := *buf*[*front*]; *front* := *front* **mod** *n* + 1

The **mod** (modulo) operator is employed to guarantee that the values of *front* and *rear* are always between 1 and *n*. The queue or buffered messages is, therefore, stored in slots from *buf*[*front*] up to but not including *buf*[*rear*], with *buf* treated as a circular array in which *buf*[1] follows *buf*[*n*].

Moreover, that security access is a critical issue in insuring accountability in development projects in African countries is hardly a matter of dispute. Consequently, *monitors* can be useful in this regard. As Andrews states, monitors are program modules that provide more structure than conditional critical regions yet can be implemented efficiently as semaphores. First, monitors are a data abstraction mechanism: they encapsulate the representations of abstract resources and provide a set of operations that are the *only* means by which the representation is manipulated. Particularly, a monitor contains variables that store the resource's state and procedures that implement operations on the resource. Thus, a process can access the variables in a monitor only by calling one of the monitor procedures. By ensuring that execution of procedures in the same monitor is not overlapped, mutual exclusion is provided (Andrews 1991:263).

Since a monitor places a wall around both the variables and the procedures that implement a shared resource, a monitor declaration has the following form (Andrews 1991:264:

> **monitor** *Mname*
>> declarations of permanent variables; initialization code
>> **procedure** op_1 *(formals$_1$)* body of op_1 **end**
>> ...
>> **procedure** op_n *(formals$_n$)* body of op_n **end**
> **end**

The permanent variables represent the state of the resource. They are referred to as permanent variables because they exist and retain their values as long as the monitor exists. The procedures implement the operations on the resource.

As a consequence of being an abstract type, a monitor has three significant properties. First, only the procedure names can be seen outside the monitor—they are the gates through the monitor wall. Second, the procedures within a monitor may access only the permanent variables and their parameters and local variables. Finally, permanent variables are initialized before any procedure body is executed (Andrews 1991:264-5).

This approach is very useful in cases where there are multiple producers and consumers of goods and services in an African country. A producer could be delayed waiting for an empty slot, then a consumer could fetch a message and awaken the delayed producer. However, before a producer gets a turn to execute, another producer could enter *deposit* and fill the empty slot. A similar situation could occur with consumers. It, therefore, behooves one to recheck the delay condition.

Conclusion

For many years, concurrent programming has been the exclusive domain of system programmers building operating systems or database systems. But with the increasing prevalence of multiprocessor architectures, many application programmers can now write concurrent programs to solve real world problems, as demonstrated in the preceding sections.

To facilitate writing concurrent programs, manufacturers of scientific workstations and multiprocessors provide subroutine libraries supporting process creation and a subset of the synchronization mechanisms that can be used for the problems described in this paper. One can also write a concurrent program for a specific machine by starting with a sequential program and then using a subroutine library for process creation, synchronization, and communication. A much more attractive approach is to use a high-level concurrent programming language, while one concentrates on the logic of the application and the implementors of the language deal with how to use the low-level library routines of a specific machine.

Chapter 6

A Relational Model of Data

Following the conventional analytical approach for examining the relational model of data, the current chapter is divided into six sections. The first section contains an introduction to the concept of relation in databases. The second section presents the formal definition of the relational model. The third and fourth sections extend and refine this definition by introducing, respectively, the notion of an integrity constraint, as a means for modeling specific aspects of the application, and some operators on relations, which form the basis for an algebra used to query databases. The fifth section discusses the notions of flat and nested relations, clarifying the kinds of relations considered in the relational model. Finally, the sixth section presents an introduction to normal forms, which make up one of the most important topics in the theoretical study of databases.

Relations in Databases

Brathwaite provides a basic definition of *relations* as "a set of two- dimensional tables...required in the normalization process"—i.e. a process used to transform data into information (1991:68-68). He also offers the following as other definitions of data normalization:

(1) The union of relations R and S is the set of all attributes contained in either R or S or in both. RS is used to denote the union of relations R and S.

(2) The intersection of relations R and S is the set of all attributes contained in both R and S. RS is used to denote the intersection of relations R and S.

(3) The difference of relations R and S is the set of all attributes contained in relation R but not in relation S. R - S is used to denote the difference of relations R and S.

(4) A decomposition of a relation R is a set of relations R such that the union of relations R is the relation R (Brathwaite 1991:69):

Date and Darwen ask the following question: If it is true that a relational database is basically just a database in which the data are perceived as tables, then why exactly is such a database referred to as relational? They then provide the answer that a "Relation is just a mathematical term for a table...a table of a certain specific kind...." (1992:7).

In informal contexts, suggest Date and Darwen, it is usual to treat the concepts *relation* and *table* as if they were synonymous, since the term *table* is employed more frequently than the term *relation* in such contexts. They provide the following explanation for why the latter concept (i.e. *relation*) was introduced in the first place (1992:7-8):

(1)   Relational systems are based on what is called *the relational model of data*.

(2)   The relational model, in turn, is an abstract theory that is based on certain aspects of mathematics (specifically, set theory and predicate logic).

(3)   The principles of the relational model were originally laid down in 1969-1970 by one man, Dr. E. F. Codd, at that time a researcher in IBM. It was late in 1968 that Codd, a mathematician by training, first realized that the discipline of mathematics could be used to inject some solid principles and rigor into a field—database management—that, prior to that time, was all too deficient in any such qualities....Since that time, those ideas (by now almost universally accepted) have had a wide- ranging influence on just about every aspect of database technology, and indeed on other fields as well, such as the field of artificial intelligence and natural language processing.

Date and Darwen also point out that the relational model as originally conceived by Codd very deliberately and utilized concepts, such as the term *relation* itself, that were not familiar in data processing circles at the time. These concepts were very fuzzy. In other words, they lacked the needed precision to delineate the type of formal theory for which Codd was advocating (1992:8).

Date and Darwen also offer the following categories into which the different kinds of *relations* can be sensibly placed (1992:51):

(1) First, a *named* relation is simply a relation that has been declared to the DBMS by some suitable authorized user; the declaration will include a relation name, of course. In current systems, the named relations are the base relations and the views....

(2) Second, an *expressible* relation is a relation that can be obtained from the set of named relations by means of an expression of the relational algebra (or whatever language is provided by the DBMS for writing relation-valued expressions). Of course, every named relation is an expressible relation, but the converse is not true. Base relations, views, snapshots, and query results are all expressible relations.

(3) Third, a *stored* relation is an expressible relation (*not* necessarily a named relation...) that is supported by the DBMS in some "direct, efficient" manner. (With appropriate definitions of "direct" and "efficient," of course...).

(4) ...A *base* relation is a named relation that is not expressible in terms of other named relations.

(5) *derived* relation is an expressible relation that is not a base relation. Views—and snapshots—are thus named derived relations. Query results are unnamed derived relations. And a base relation is a named relation that is not a derived relation.

In light of the forgoing classification of the different kinds of relations, Date and Darwen suggest that it is only natural that the set of stored relations must be such that all named relations and, therefore, all expressible relations can be derived from them. However, they caution that *"there is no requirement that all stored relations be base relations, nor that all base relations be stored relations"* (1992:51).

Unlike Date and Darwen (1992), Grill introduces the concept of *relation* in two ways: diagrammatically and mathematically. Diagrammatically, a relation is graphically depicted as nothing more than a simple table which is made up of rows and columns. He refers to the columns of the table as *domains,* akin to the language of relational algebra, and the rows as *tuples.* Thus, for Grill, a data file is a relation only when the following attributes are evident (1990:56-67):

(1) Each row in the table corresponds exactly with a data file. Each record in the data file can be uniquely identified ie no 2 identical records exist in it (sic).

(2) Each column in the table corresponds exactly with a data element name of the record type. One and the same name may not be repeated in the record type.

(3) The intersection point of the i tuple and the j domain contains the value V_{ij}. This is the value assumed by the j data element of the record type in the i record of the data file.

(4) A tuple variable t is a variable to which one can allocate one row of the table as a value. t can be compared with an input buffer into which one record of the data file will be entered.

Grill shows that, mathematically, a relation R is a subset of the Cartesian product of the sets W_1, W_2,...W_m. Thus,

$$RfW_1 \times W_2 \times ...W_m$$

where the set W_j comprises all the different values which can be assumed by the data element D_j in the relation R (1990:57). The rules by which the Cartesian product is constructed is beyond the scope of the current study.

Yang introduces an architecture of a database management system (DBMS) that seems to fit with a large number of other DMBSs. His architecture is divided into the following three levels (1986:12):

(1) Conceptual level—This level is referred to as the *conceptual* or *logical database*. It is located between the other two levels. It consists of the abstract representation of the database (i.e., independent from the physical implementation).

(2) Internal level—This lowest level is referred to as the *physical* or *internal database* that is the implementation of the logical database. It is concerned with data types, record formats, storage structures, and access methods. It represents the database as actually stored and retrieved.

(3) External level—This highest level is referred to as the *external database*. It is concerned with the views created from the logical database by users. Each view consists of some portion of the logical database.

Therefore, for Yang, a DBMS is a software system capable of managing the preceding three levels and other pertinent interfaces.

Yang notes that a model of databases, conventionally known as a *data model*, is primarily employed for modeling a logical database that is the most important part in the design of a DBMS. These data models include the entity-relationship, the network model, the hierarchical model, the relational model, and many more (1986:12-13).

Yang also points out that, in addition to freedom from the frustrations of having to deal with the clutter of the details of storage structures and access methods from the user interface, the relational model offers other important advantages. One of them is simplicity. Since the user is presented with simple and consistent tabular relations, simplicity is achieved. Another is that the relational model has a sound theoretical base. Since it rests on the well-developed mathematical theory of relations and the first-order logic, the relational model is mathematically rigorous. This strong theoretical foundation makes it possible to use the relational model to design and evaluate relational databases by using systematic methods based on abstractions which, in turn, can enable one to concentrate on general approaches, to reduce complexities, and to assist in comprehension (1963:13). It is not surprising, therefore, that the relational model has provided the architectural focus for the design of databases and some general purpose DBMS—e.g., INGRES, PROLOG, and SYSTEM R.

In addition, Yang mentions that the term *field* refers to the smallest item of data that has real-world meaning in the file management system of an operation system. This item, he points out, possesses a specific data type, such as integer, floating point number, or character string and requires a number of bytes of storage space to be specified. This item is also assigned a name. And, as Yang notes, a field is the smallest typed and named data item. Thus, he suggests, in a relational database, each relation is represented by a table, and each column of a tabular relation equals a field (1986:13).

Yang further suggests that, in a relational database, a table represents each relation. Attributes, he notes, are simply the symbols employed to differentiate and label the columns of the table denoting a relation. Thus, he maintains, a field or column name is no more than an attribute. And that all attributes appearing in a table must de distinct and included in the universe U. In essence, attributes are global in a relational database in the sense that an attribute appearing in any two distinct tables of a relational database must carry the same meaning. Hence, for Yang, any table of a relational database must involve only a non-empty subset of U. Consequently, according to him, attributes must be time-invariant in the sense that their values should be more or less independent of time (1986:14). Yang provides the following example to clarify his proposition:

> [A] personnel database having AGE as an attribute to indicate the ages of employees would be different AGE-values for any employee from year to year, whereas the value of the attribute DATEOFBIRTH for each employee would have the property of time-independence, and the current age of an employee would be easily computed from the date of birth of the employee and the value of the current year. Use of DATEOFBIRTH rather than AGE as an attribute is a better choice (1986:14).

Yang goes on to suggests that, in order to prevent the occurrence of an infinite relation, each domain is necessarily kept finite. This is one reason, according to him, that each domain is defined as a finite set of values. He also points out that, although attributes are time-invariant, an insertion into, an update of, or a deletion from any table of a relational database results into a different table, implying a different relational database (1986:15).

Another aspect Yang points out about a file management system of an operating system is a *record*, which he defines as "a set of related fields treated as a single unit for storage and retrieval." Yang adds that, since its fields have specific data types, a record has a specific format. The rows in a tabular relation, he suggests, are similar to records and are conventionally referred to in relational databases as *tuples*. However, Yang makes it very clear that the definition of these tuples is not the same as that of the tuples in mathematics called, appropriately, *mathematical tuples* (1986:16).

Thus, an economic development database must be an integrated collection of persistent data, representing the information of interest to policy-makers for the various programs that use them: data can be described autonomously, and programs can make use of the descriptions. This approach will make it possible for different programs to access and modify the same database and share common data, thereby reducing inconsistencies and redundancies among the representations of the same data in different programs.

As such, the economic development relational model suggested in this study successfully couples a precise mathematical definition with a useful representation based on tables. The relational database is represented as a collection of tables. Each table is assigned a unique name in the database. A row in a table represents a relationship among sets of values. Column headings contain distinct names, and for each column a set of possible values exist, referred to as *domain*. Figure 1 shows the tabular representation of some information about development projects and project coordinators for a development program.

Development project

ProjectCode	ProjectDirect-or	ProjectType	Expenditure
01	Aaaa	Nutrition	$8m
02	Bbbb	Education	$10m
03	Cccc	Health	$8m
04	Dddd	Shelter	$10m

Project coordinator

Coordinator	ProjectCode	NumberServed
Eeee	01	4m
Ffff	02	2m
Gggg	03	3m
Hhhh	04	4m

Figure 1: The tabular representation of a database

Each row in the preceding tables is an ordered n-tuples of values $<d_1, d_2,...,d_n>$ such that each value dj is in the domain of the jth column, for j = 1,2,...,n, where n is the number of columns. The number of n-tuples in the relation is the cardinality of the relation.

> **Example 1:** By means of a relation, information about the various project divisions for an economic development program is represented as follows. This relation is called *development*:
>
>   *development ⊆ string x string x date x date*
>   *development* = {<Aaaa, Nutrition, Jan-02-95, Dec-31-95>,
>   <Bbbb, Education, Jan-02-95, Dec-31-95>,
>   <Cccc, Health, Jan-02-95, Dec-31-95>,
>   <Dddd, Shelter, Jan-02-95, Dec-31-95>}

In the relation, the domain *date* has two distinct roles to indicate: respectively, the dates groups of projects start and end. The only way to distinguish between them is the fact that they are respectively the third and fourth domains in the sequence. The same happens to the domain *string*.

Example 2: In considering the data in example 1, the following attributes can be introduced:

Project Coordinator	with *dom(ProjectsCoordinator)*	= *string*
Project Types	with *dom(ProjectTypes)*	= *string*
Beginning	with *dom(Beginning)*	= *date*
End	with *dom(End)*	= *date*

The tuple <Aaaa, Nutrition, Jan-02-95, Dec-31-95> can be described by means of the function *t* such that *t[ProjectsCoordinator]* = Aaaa, *t[ProjectTypes]* = Nutrition, *t[Beginning]* = Jan-02-95, *t[End]* = Dec-31- 95.

Since it is possible that not all aspects of the application to be represented in the database are known, it is reasonable to assert that a relation contains values not specified at the moment. Taking this into account, the domains of relations can be extended by adding the so-called *null value*, which represents the absence of information: it is indicated by the symbol .

Formal Definition of the Relational Model

Based upon Codd's work, Yang defines the relational model of databases as follows (1986:29):

(1) a set of time-varying relations...with time-invariant schemes...,

(2) the insert-update-delete rules, and

(3) data sublanguage at least as powerful as the relational algebra.

Yang further suggests that closely associated with the relational model are a variety of normalization concepts that are semantic in nature, being time-invariant properties of time-varying relations. Examples of such concepts, according to Yang, are functional dependencies, multivalued dependencies, lossless nature joins, and various normal forms. In addition, he points out, Codd proposed various extensions to the relational model of databases in order to capture more meaning (1986:29).

For Date and Darwen, a good way to characterize the relational model of data is a way of looking at data. Put differently, it is (a) a prescription for a manner of presenting data—namely, by means of tables; and (b) a prescription for a manner of manipulating data presentation—namely, by means of operators such as *join*. More precisely, these authors add, the relational model is concerned with three aspects of data: (1) data *structure*, (2) data *integrity*, and (3) data *manipulation*. They also caution that the relational model is a theory; however, it is not necessary for a system to support the theory in its entirety in order to qualify as relational according to the definition (1992:9).

According Gardarin and Valduriez, the relational model is based on three principal concepts derived from set theory. The first concept is *domain*—a set of values specified by a name. Domains are sets of data values that are used to model data. Like sets, Gardarin and Valduriez suggest, domains can be defined extensionally by enumerating the constituent values, or intensionally by defining a distinctive property of the value of the domain. The second concept is *relation*—a subset of the Cartesian product of a list of domains characterized by a name. Thus, as a subset of a Cartesian product, a relation is made up of tuples. And according to Gardarin and Valduriez, and as also mentioned earlier, the convenient way to display a relation is via a two-dimensional table. Each line is the result of a tuple and each column to a domain of the Cartesian product that is being considered. To distinguish between the columns and to disregard their classification order while enabling the existence of several columns for a domain, a name must be assigned to each column. This aspect of a column of a relation designated by a name refers to the third concept—i.e. *attribute*. The name given an attribute is critical in that it often differs from that of the domain, which may be perceived as the attribute medium (1989:92-93).

Additionally, Gardarin and Valduriez point out that a relational model makes it possible for one to manipulate data values that change over time. They further suggest that relations change with time because tuples are added, modified, or deleted during the lifetime of a database. They also make the point that the structure of a relation described in terms of relation name, domains, and attributes is invariant for a given relation. This invariant structure is defined in the *relation schema* as the name of the relation proceeded by the list of its attributes with their attendant domains (1989:95).

Like Gardarin and Valduriez, Brathwaite characterizes the relational model of data as a two-dimensional table. He adds that the data represented in the figure comprise a *relation*. Each column in the table is called an *attribute*. The values in the column are derived from a domain or set of all possible values. The rows of the table are referred to as *tuples* (Brathwaite 1991:25).

The advantages of a relational data model, according to Brathwaite, are as follows (1991:26):

(1) *Simplicity*: The end user is presented with a simple data model. His or her requests are formulated in terms of the information content and do not reflect any complexities caused by system-oriented aspects. A relational data model is what the user sees, but it is not necessarily what will be implemented physically.

(2) *Nonprocedural requests*: Because there is no positional dependency between the relations, requests do not have to reflect any preferred structure and therefore can be nonprocedural.

(3) *Data independence*: This should be one of the major objectives of any DBMS. The relational data model removes the details of storage structure and access strategy from the user interface. The model provides a relatively higher degree of data independence than do the next two models. To be able to make use of this property of the relational data model, however, the design of the relations must be complete and accurate.

Brathwaite also discusses eight types of operators in the relational data model. These operators, according to him, are those that are found in relational algebra; they do not operate on individual rows but on entire tables, and they always yield tables as results. The characteristics of these operators are summarized as follows (Brathwaite 1991:27-31):

(1) The Union Operator combines rows from two similar tables to four new tables. The new tables contain the rows that are in either or both of the original tables.

(2) The Intersection Operator combines the rows from two similar tables to form a new table that contains the rows that are in both of the original tables.

(3) The Difference Operator combines two tables to produce a third table that contains all rows that are in the first table but not in the second.

(4) The Product Operator combines the rows from two dissimilar tables to for a new table. In this case the third table is formed by concatenating each row of the first table with each row of the second table.

(5) The Select Operator produces a second table from the original table based on a selection criteria (sic).

(6) The Project Operator produces a new table that contains all the rows from the original table but only a subset of columns.

(7) The Join Operator combines the rows from two tables to form a third. The resulting table is formed in such a way that in each row the data values from the columns on which the join is based have the same data values.

(8) The divide operator compares the data values in columns from the two tables and produces a third that eliminates the columns that have equal volumes.

Indeed, Brathwaite's discourse provides a clear picture of how data structures form the building blocks of the relational model. It also highlights the fact that relational DBMSs hinge upon solid algebraic theory.

For Simovici and Tenney, a relational database can be informally viewed as a collection of tables. Thus, they insist that, in the process of defining relational databases, one must provide a precise definition of the notion of table. In contemplation, these scholars identify the following elements of a table (1995:25):

(1) the name of the table,

(2) the heading of the table, and

(3) the set of rows of the tables.

And to formalize the notion of a table, Simovici and Tenney suggest the following (1995:26):

> ...begin from a set U that is a collection of symbols called *relational attributes*. For each symbol A U, we assume that there exists a set Dom(A) called the *domain of A*. The symbol A represents a title of a column in a table, and Dom(A) specifies the values that can occur in that column. We assume henceforth that the domain of every attribute contains at least two elements. Note that if there were only one element a in Dom(A), any column that corresponds to A would have only a in it and thus never convey any useful information.

In light of the preceding discussion, it is quite evident that a data model can be utilized as a formal tool for describing information of interest for an economic development application. And according to Atzeni and De Antonellis, there are two possible description levels (1993:6):

1. The intensional level, involving the general property of classes of values and classes of correspondences among them.

2. The extensional level, involving the actual values and correspondences between them.

In addition, Atzeni and De Antonellis state that in the relational model the intensional level corresponds to the time variant description of relations (schemes) while the extensional level corresponds to the contents of relations (instances) at a given moment (1993:6).

> **Example 3:** Considering the information on development projects and project coordinators in Figure 1, the database scheme contains two relation schemes as follows:

DEVELOPMENTPROJECT
   ProjectCode, ProjectDirector, ProjectType, Expenditure)

PROJECTCOORDINATOR
   (Coordinator, ProjectCode, NumberServed)

The relation instances shown in Figure 1 are
   developmentproject = $\{t_1, t_2, t_3, t_4\}$
   projectcoordinator = $\{t_5, t_6, t_7, t_8\}$

where t_1 *[ProjectCode]* = 01, t_1 *[ProjectDirector]* = Aaaa, t_1 *[ProjectType]* = Nutrition, t_1 *[Expenditure]* = \$8m, and so on.

Integrity Constraints

"Integrity rules," assert Gardarin and Valduriez, "are assertions that the data contained in the database must satisfy" (1989:96). Theese scholars also point out that one can distinguish between structural rules, which are part and parcel of the data model, and the behavioral rules proper to a particular application. They note that the relational model enforces a structural rule that is the uniqueness of key. They also state that it is convenient and usual to add two other types of structural rules—namely, the entity and referential constraints. All three types of integrity constraints—i.e. key, entity, and referential, Gardarin and Valduriez say, make up the minimum integrity rules that should be supported by any relational DBMS (1989:96).

Gardarin and Valduriez go on to explicate these integrity constraints further. In terms of the uniqueness of key, they suggest that a relation by definition refers to a set of tuples. Since a set lacks duplicate elements, the same tuple cannot exist more than once in a relation. To identify the relation's tuples without providing all the attribute values and efficiency and to check the absence of duplicate tuples in a relation, they suggest that the concept of *key* is employed. They then provide a more general definition of a *key* as a "minimal set of attributes whose values identify a unique tuple in a relation" (1989:96). More formally, Gardarin and Valduriez define a *key* as follows:

A key of a relation *R* is a set of attributes *K* such that:
* For any tuple *t*1 and *t*2 of any instance of *R*, *t*1 (*K*) *t*2 (*K*)
* There does not exist any proper subset of *K* having the previous property (1989:96).

Gardarin and Valduriez maintain that for convenience, a set of attributes with a key is referred to as a *superkey*. They note that each relation has at least one key, and that the knowledge of all the attribute values composing this key is tantamount to a unique tuple in the relation. They add that when several keys are present, they are referred to as *candidate keys*. Furthermore, they point out that one of the keys is arbitrarily selected and referred to as the *primary key* and the rest are referred to as the *alternative keys*. They conclude by stating that the concept of key is germane to a relation's intension—i.e. all possible extensions. And that two tuples with the same value cannot exist in any relation's extentions; thus, the choice of key must be the outcome of a semantic study of the relation—i.e. all possible extensions and not only a particular one (1989:96).

As for referential constraints, Gardarin and Valduriez suggest that a relational model is often employed to mimic real-life entities that are objects with their own existence and relationships between these objects. These entities, they point out, often correspond to nouns, and relationships model verbs. They note that there exist different ways of representing entities and relationships as relations. They are as follows: "In a simple representation, an entity occurrence corresponds to a tuple in a relation; such a tuple is composed of a key that is the entity key; the entity properties are expressed as tuple attributes. A relationship type is generally modeled by a relation whose attributes represent the keys of the particular entities, as well as the relationship's own properties" (1989:96-97).

Formally, then, Gardarin and Valduriez define a *referential constraint* as an "integrity constraint applied to a relation $R1$ asserting that the value of a set of attributes in $R1$ must be equal to a key value in a relation $R2$" (1989:98). Consequently, they suggest that

> The set of attributes in $R1$ is called a *foreign key*. Such an integrity constraint is generally applied to relationships. A relationship can exist only if the participating entity instances are already recorded in the corresponding relations. Note that in the definition, $R1$ and $R2$ are not necessarily distinct; the constraint can be applied to two tuples of the same relation, Except when the relationship is functional, a foreign key in a relation $R1$ is a part of $R1$'s key because relationship keys include the keys of the participating entities (Gardarin and Valduriez 1989:98).

In essence, by specifying the foreign keys, referential constraints can be defined.

As far as entity constraint is concerned, Gardarin and Valduriez first examine the notion of null values. According to them, frequently an attribute is unknown or inapplicable when inserting tuples in a relation. As a consequence, they suggest, one must introduce a conventional value in the relation to represent an unknown or inapplicable attribute. This is called the *null value*, defined as a "conventional value introduced in a relation to represent an unknown or inapplicable attribute value" (1989:98).

Gardarin and Valduriez further point out that the exact significance of a null values is often ambiguous. It cannot be applied to all the attributes of a relation. One must know about the existence of a key to verify that this particular key does not already exist. Thus, these scholars suggest, one of the structural constraints of the relational model is the *entity constraint*, which they define as an "integrity constraint compelling all participating attributes of a primary key to being not null" (1989:98). And for Gardarin and Valduriez, the relational model does not compel foreign keys not belonging to a primary key to be not null if it is not specified otherwise by a domain definition constraint. This, they say, can provide some flexibility in the model (1989:98-99).

In addition to constraints imposed on attributes, domain, tuples, and relations, Yang suggests that there are many other constraints. He classifies these constraints into two major types as follows (1986:22):

(1)   One type of constraint specifies the characteristics of an attribute (including its domain) independent of any other attributes in a database....These are related to the semantics of the values in domains.

(2)   The other type of constraint specifies a relationship among several attributes (i.e., a relation among several domains of attributes) in a database. This type of constraints is related to the structure of a database....These constraints are called *functional dependencies* in general and *key dependencies* in particular.

To design a good database, Yang suggests that one may need to (1) collect enough practical data; (2) choose appropriate attributes and their domains; (3) propose relation schemes; (4) find data dependencies, particularly the key dependency for each relation scheme; (5) reduce dependencies; and (6) eliminate anomalies that result form insertion, deletion, and updates, etc. He further points out that entity-relationship diagrams established in the entity-relationship data model can be valuable in solving a part of the problem during the initial state (1986:26).

Furthermore, Yang notes that each tuple or relation has a specific set of attributes as its scheme, and a database possesses a specific set of subsets of attributes as its scheme. He mentions that a tuple, relation, or database also has a specific set of constraints. And that a minimum set of attributes, referred to as a *key* for a relation, is one of the fundamental and vital constraints. Thus, Yang argues, defining a relation scheme only by a set of attributes is not enough, as a set of data dependencies is another important component of the definition (1986:26).

Yang also suggests that a hypergraph can be employed to graphically represent a database scheme. One can represent the attributes by vertices, and s/he can represent each relation scheme by a hyperedge. In sketching a hypergraph, Yang also suggests that one label the vertices or nodes by the attributes in U and represent the hyperedge by a closed curve enclosing the attributes of a relation scheme. In addition to hypergraphs, this scholar also suggest the use of decomposition trees for vertical normalization, entity- relationship diagrams such as CAZ-graphs (i.e. combined ACOVER and ZCOVER) for a relation scheme, and FD (functional dependency)-graphs to design a database scheme based on functional dependencies to provide a synthesis algorithm (1986:27-28).

As Date and Darwen argue, certain critical aspects of the relational model—in particular, all aspects dealing with *data integrity*—are relevant only because of the "time-varying" nature of relations within the model. The general point, these scholars say, is that integrity constraints (or most of them, anyway) must by definition apply "for all time"—i.e. to every possible value of the body of a relation. Thus, they suggest, the concepts of *candidate key, primary key, alternate key,* and *foreign key*—all of which are essentially integrity-related constructs—derive their meanings only within the context of "time-varying" relations (1992:48).

And according to Brathwaite, the relational model is generally perceived to be weak on integrity constraints. He states that entity integrity and referential integrity are the two standard constraints that are now considered to be part of the relational model. He also points out that commercial DBMSs implement entity integrity through the key constraint by not allowing null values on a key attribute. Unfortunately, he notes, many relational DBMSs combine the specification of a key with that of a physical index. And that while referential integrity has not been generally available in relational DBMSs, some of the newer DBMSs such as DB2, however, are making it possible to specify this integrity (1991:169).

Furthermore, Brathwaite points out that the hierarchical model has the built-in hierarchical constraints that a record type can possess at most one real parent in a hierarchy. He mentions that other constraints can be found in each individual DBMSs. For example, he notes that IMS makes provision for only one virtual parent for a record type. He adds that there is no provision to enforce consistency among duplicate records; enforcement must be effected by the application programs that update the databases. Consequently, he notes, the implicit constraint that a child record must be related to a parent record is enforced; and that also, child records are automatically erased when their parent or ancestor is erased (1991:169).

Also, according to Brathwaite, the network model is the richest among the three implementation models vis-a-vis the types of constraints it specifies and enforces. The set retention option, he points out, specifies constraints on the behavior of member records in a set with respect to the owner record—e.g., whether every record must have an owner or not. In addition, Brathwaite suggests that

> Automatic set types with SET SELECTION BY STRUCTURAL match the key field of an owner with a field in the member record. The CHECK option can be used to specify a similar constraint for MAN-UAL nonautomatic set types. Key constraints are specified by a DUPLICATES NOT ALLOWED clause. Hence, many structural constraints on relationship types can be specified to a network DBMS (1991:169-170).

More concretely, Simovici and Tenney present techniques used in Structured Query Language (SQL) to implement some of the constraints discussed above. As these scholars caution, not all constraints can be dealt with in SQL. For some, one must write the code in the applications that utilize the database. When possible, they note, one must use the database system itself to enforce constraint. This will insure coherence among various database applications, avoid repeating the definition of the constraints and, thus, help simplify the code of the database applications (1995:254).

SQL92, according to Simovici and Tenney, describes constraints by employing *constraints descriptors*—they can be either *table constraint descriptors* or *assertion descriptors*, in consonance with the types of constraints SQL92 identifies. They also note that an *assertion* is a named constraint that is not pegged to any table. As such, each constraint is either *deferrable* or *nondeferrable*, relating to the idea of transaction—i.e. a sequence of SQL statements that is executed as a whole. Put differently, Simovici and Tenney say that "either the effect of every statement of the transaction is made permanent, or no statement has any effect on the database" (1995:254). In essence, according to these scholars, if a constraint is nondeferrable, then it is checked at the end of each SQL statement of a transaction. Those constraints that are deferrable can be checked at the end of the transactions (1995:254-255).

Moreover, as Atzeni and De Antonellis observe, in many cases, it is not true that any finite set of tuples can be an acceptable relation, in terms of its interpretation, even if the tuples have the right degree and the component values belong to the domains of the respective attribute (1993:8-9)

> **Example 4:** Consider the relation in Figure 2, which refers to the information about employees in a development training program. Here, it is clearly unreasonable to have an employee who is 140 years old; also, in all organizations, the Employee Number is a unique identifier for each employee, and it is thus impossible

to have two employees with the same value for the attribute *Employee #*.

Employment

Employee	Employee#	Age
Iiii	2945	30
Jjjj	6582	140
Kkkk	6582	35

Figure 2: A relation with impossible values

Thus, modeling the application also calls for identifying the properties that must be respected by the tuples in the database, so that they can lead to correct interpretations. Consequently, the concept of *integrity constraint* is introduced to model the properties that must be satisfied by all the instances of a relational scheme.

As Atzeni and De Antonellis point out, since relations are sets, no relation contains two identical tuples; thus, for each relation, the set of all its attributes is a superkey. Therefore, according to these scholars, each relation has at least one key. In addition, they note, a key constitutes the assertion of a property that must be valid for all acceptable (with respect to the application of interest) instances of a relation scheme: it is an integrity constraint on the relation scheme (1993:10).

> **Example 5:** Suppose a project director wants to handle data about employees; for each of them, s/he is interested in National Number (NN), last name, date of birth, Employee Number, and project. Therefore, s/he uses a relation whose scheme has the name *EMPLOYEES*, and the attributes *NN, LastName, BirthDate, Employee#, Project*. Clearly, since no pair of employees

has identical Nns or Employee Numbers, both *NN* and *Employee#* are superkeys for every acceptable relation over this scheme and are therefore considered superkeys for the scheme itself. Also, if one assumes that no pair of employees with the same name was born on the same day, one has that the set of attributes {*LastName, BirthDate*} is also a superkey for the scheme. Moreover, all of them are minimal and thus are indeed keys. For the first two, the fact is trivial; as regards {*LastName, BirthDate*}, it follows from the fact that neither names nor birth dates are unique. An example relation over this scheme is exhibited in Figure 3. Note that in the figure, the attribute *BirthDate* also allows a unique identification of the tuples in the relation; however, this is just coincidental, since it need not happen for all the relations over the scheme.

If null values are allowed, argue Atzeni and De Antonellis, then the definition of unique identification is relaxed and refers only to tuples that have no null values on the set of attributes involved. Therefore, these scholars add, no restriction is imposed on the tuples that have null values in the key, leading to some undesirable situations (1993:11).

Employees

NN	LastName	BirthDate	Employee#	Project
11111	Aata	Jun-6-1952	4497	Rice
22222	Bata	Apr-4-1960	7970	Adult Education
33333	Cata	Nov-29-1955	8999	Rice
44444	Data	Jul-27-1960	1120	Nursing
55555	Aata	Jun-16-1951	3850	Housing

Figure 3: A relation with various keys

Example 6: Consider the scheme in Example 5 and the first relation in Figure 4. Here the first tuple has null values on each key, and it is therefore impossible to identify it in any way. If one is to add to the relation another tuple with *LastName* equal to Bata, s/he does not know whether it refers to the same employee ro to another one. A similar problem emerges in the second relation in Figure 4: even if each tuple has a non-null value on at least one key, one does not know whether the two tuples refer to the same employee or to two different employees.

Employees

NN	LastName	BirthDate	Employee #	Project
z	Bata	z	z	Adult Education
33333	Cata	Nov-29-1953	z	Rice

Employees

NN	LastName	BirthDate	Employee #	Project
z	Aata	Jun-6-1962	4497	Rice
55555	Aata	z	z	Rice

Figure 4: Relations with null values for the keys

Example 6 clearly shows that some restrictions should be placed on the possible appearance of null values in the keys. The easiest solution that allows a unique identification of each tuple in the relation, according to Atzeni and De Antonellis, is as follows: "select one of the keys of the relation (the *primary key*), and require that each tuple be null-free on the attributes of the primary key" (1993:11).

Example 7: In the *EMPLOYEES* relation scheme, it is reasonable to require that *Employee#* be the primary key. Thus, the relations in Figure 4 are not allowed, whereas the relation in Figure 5 is allowed (as well as the relation in Figure 3, which contains no null values).

Employees

NN	LastName	BirthDate	Employee #	Project
z	Bata	z	7970	Adult Education
z	Bata	z	3321	Rice
33333	Cata	Nov-29-1955	8999	Rice

Figure 5: A relation with a (null-free) primary key

A notion related to that of keys that has practical importance is a *foreign key* because it provides a way of relating tuples of distinct relations. Atzeni and De Antonellis define a foreign key this way: "A subset X of the attributes of a relation r_1 is a *foreign key* of r_1 if the values of the tuples of r_1 on X are values of the primary key of some other relation r_2 " (1993:12).

Thus, as Brathwaite suggests, one must implement many-to-many relationships as two one-to-many relationships when creating a new table with a primary key consisting of a concatenation of primary keys of the other two tables. If this type of relationship has attributes, Brathwaite maintains that they will become attributes (columns) of the newly created table. Each primary key column then becomes a foreign key in the new table and references the primary key of the corresponding entity (1991:46).

Example 8: Consider the scheme of the database in Example 3. Primary keys of the relation schemes *DEVELOPMENTPRO-JECT* and *PROJECTCOORDINATOR* are, respectively,

ProjectCode and *ProjectDirector, ProjectCode.* In the *ProjectCoordinator* relation *ProjectCode* is a foreign key since its values are values of the primary key of the *DEVELOPMENT-PROJECT* relation. For a given value of *ProjectCode* in the *projectcoordinator* relation, it is possible to consult the *development-project* relation to find information associated with that value.

Query Languages

According to Simovici and Tenney, query languages facilitate interaction between users of database systems. The query language of a DBMS entails two major functions: (1) to define the data structures that serve as receptacles for the data of the database, and (2) to facilitate the speedy retrieval and modification of data. Consequently, two component of a query language are distinguished by Simovici and Tenney: (1) *data definition component* and (2) *data manipulation component* (1995:3).

A query, then, Simovici and Tenney suggest, is a way to retrieve data from the tables of a database. From the perspective of the DBMS, they say, a query is a program whose compilation and execution are imperative. Consequently, a query is put through the usual phases of programming processing: lexical analysis, parsing (syntactic analysis), validation (semantic analysis), and code generation. Conceptually, Simovici and Tenney suggest and describe the following components which a subsystem of a DBMS that is in charge of a query execution consists (195:399-340):

(1) The *query compiler* performs the lexical and syntactical analysis of the query. It also validates the query, i.e., it checks whether the tables, views, indexes, and attributes in the query actually exist and that they are used appropriately.

(2) The *query optimizer* chooses one alternative among several alternatives for executing a query.

(3) The *code generator* transforms the execution plan chosen by the query optimizer into an executable program.

(4) The *routine component* executes the resultant query program.

Simovici and Tenney further maintain that the query optimizer considers the resources required by each execution plan when evaluating and comparing various alternative executions. CPU time and the number of input/output operations comprise the vital resources in this process (1995:400). Since compilers have been thoroughly dealt with in computer science literature, Simovici and Tenney then go on to focus on issues dealing with query optimization—i.e. algebraic manipulation, selection query processing, join processing, the Wong-Youssefi Algorithm, and informed decisions.

As it pertains to algebraic manipulation, Simovici and Tenney state that relational algebra makes available a convenient model for discussing the logic of query execution and provides some insight into the physical-level operations that tield the actual answers to the queries. The computation yielded tends to compute products of tables that are small. It comes immediately after the computation of a product by a selection to eliminate tuples that are useless in the result (1995:400-404).

For selection of query processing, Simovici and Tenney concentrate on simple queries of the common form

$$T \text{ where } C,$$

where *C* is a condition. They remind readers that the conditions in a selection are defined recursively, beginning with the atomic conditions (1995:404).

In the case of join processes, Simovici and Tenney discuss several. The first, *Nested-Loops Join Algorithm*, which is the simplest algorithm for computing joins, is relatively efficient when there exists either a matching index on the inner table based on the attribute involved in the join, or when the selctivity factor, *self*, is high because each operation fetches several tuples. The second, *Sort-Merge Join Algorithm*, which eliminates the need for repeatedly scanning tables, has a major advantage over the nested-loops method. The third, *Hash-Join Algorithm*, which reduces the number of comparisons between tuples by processing only joinable tuples, determines joinability by employing the hashing function *h*. The fourth is *Computing the Join of Several Tables* through which, ceteris paribus, the first plan is executed and so on. Other factor, nonetheless, such as the storage structures of the tables, also determine the decision. The fifth, *Subquery Processing*, through which the database must evaluate a subquery for all rows of the calling query when a subquery is being computed. Moreover, the DBMS is not allowed to use indices and to reduce the number of the tuples involved using properties of the conditions mentioned under **where** (1995:406-411).

Brathwaite also introduces several subqueries or, as he calls them, queries within queries. They are as follows: (1) *Simple Subqueries* that nest only one level of query; (2) *Multiple-Level Subqueries* that nest more than one level of subquery; (3) *Correlated Subquery* that are evaluated with respect to certain values selected by the main query—in this case, the inner query runs in correlation with the test value of the main query; (4) *Union of Two Tables* in which two or more SQL queries can be combined with the UNION operation—the UNION key word is placed between any two SELECT statements to indicate that the result tables should contain all records selected from the first and second tables; (5) *Unions of Unions* in which one is not limited to combining just two SELECT queries together— instead, one can combine more than two queries together using a UNION operation in order (1991:101-104).

And According to Simovici and Tenney, the Wong-Youssefi Algorithm was developed for queries written in QUEL (QUEry Language). This technique seeks to avoid computing the Cartesian product of full tables and to limit the number of tuples to be scanned. The paramount objective of this algorithm is to reduce a **retrieve** construct involving several variables to a sequence of queries involving one variable, a process referred to as *decomposition* (1995:412).

As for informed decisions, Simovici and Tenney reiterate the point that a typical DBMS must choose between several execution alternatives for a query. The choices, they say, are better made in the DBMS if they are informed about the tables' contents. If this information is missing, database systems use query processing techniques that are determined only by the database schema, including the presence of indices, and the results are far from optimal. DBMSs with sophisticated query processing capabilities can extract information about database tables whenever the database administrator issues specific commands (1995:419).

For Gardarin and Valduriez, relational database management systems (RDBMSs) provide high-level languages that are procedural and utilize set-at-a-time operators. To query a relational database, one must specify the desired result without providing the access paths to the data. As such, the DBMS determines how to access the data by applying a query processing algorithm that produces an access plan for a given query. A query processing module referred to as the *query processor* is employed to implement the algorithm. Indeed, designing a query processor is a tedious, but vital, exercise. Its usability, thus, hinges upon the fact that it is efficient in performing high-level queries and conditions the performance of the DBMS. Since queries are used to perform various tasks such as end-user retrieval and update queries, schema management, semantic integrity, and authorization management, the performance issue becomes very critical. Most of the criticisms that were leveled against earlier RDBMSs were for their poor performance. As to be expected, query processing methods have been redesigned and improved to be efficient over the years (1989:275).

The objective of query processing, according to Gardarin and Valduriez is to execute queries cost effectively. Choosing the best access plan to reduce cost is perceived to be computationally intractable for general queries. Thus, heuristics are imperative to minimize cost. The cost function in this context deals with machine resources such as disk space, disk input- output (IO), buffer space, and central processing unit (CPU) time. And since all query processors have an optimizing phase that exploits available access paths to data, physical database design is a pivotal issue in terms of query optimization (1989:275-276).

In terms of the objectives of query processing, Gardarin and Valduriez discuss both the problem and the function of the query key processor. They suggest that given a user query expressed in relational calculus, one will have an access to many possible strategies to perform it. While these strategies may lead to major different execution times, the main goal of the query processor is to find the optimal strategy for executing a query. And since the problem is generally NP-complete in the number of relations involved, it is, therefore, computationally intractable. Heuristics, therefore, become necessary for simplifying the problem and for finding a quasi- optimal solution (1989:276-277).

In the case of the function of the query processor, Gardarin and Valduriez point out that the role of the query process is to map a query expressed in high-level language (relational calculus) on a relational database into a sequence of lower-level operations (implementing relational algebra) acting on relations. This calls for the selection of a mapping strategy that minimizes cost: i.e. the total execution time of the query, which equals the sum of all execution times of operations that participate in the query. Gardarin and Valduriez also note that cost can also be the response time of the query; here, the objective is to maximize the parallel execution of operations. Some optimization methods strive to maximize the throughput of the entire system as measured by the number of queries processed per time unit (1989:278).

For parameters that influence query processing, Gardarin and Valduriez focus on the storage model and the complexity of database operations. According to these authors, these two aspects entail common assumptions that underlie the design of query processing algorithms in a centralized system. In terms of the storage model, they suggest that it prescribes the storage structures and algorithms supported by the system to map the conceptual schema into the physical (or internal) schema. They note that in an RDBMS, conceptual relations are generally mapped into files based upon the following two partitioning functions: (1) vertical partitioning that maps relations into files where a file corresponds to an attribute, several attributes, or the entire relation; and (2) horizontal partitioning that clusters each file based on the values of a single or multiple attributes employing a single or multiple attribute file organization (1989:279).

Gardarin and Valduriez also observe that most relational systems use an *n*-ary storage model (NSM), in which each conceptual relation is stored in a single file. The key concept in NSM, they note, is that all attributes of a conceptual tuple are stored together. This makes the vertical partitioning function quite simple. Since the horizontal partitioning function clusters all conceptual tuples of a file based on one or more attributes, several indices, also implemented as files, could be defined on nonclustered attributes. An alternative to the NSM model is the decomposition storage model (DSM), which stores all values of each attribute of a relation together in a separate file. Furthermore, a model hybrid between DSM and NSM is possible. In this case, the storage model vertically partitions a relation based on the attribute affinities such that attributes used together frequently are stored in the same file. By knowing about the most frequent queries in user workloads, one can exploit the organizational storage structures for efficient access. And since each file has several attributes and an identifier of the corresponding tuple, restrictions and projections on the groups of attributes that are frequently accessed together are the operations that are best supported by this hybrid approach. Consequently, a compromise is reached in terms of the advantages and disadvantages of both schemes. The accuracy of the vertical partitioning is paramount for achieving efficiency, according to Gardarin and Valduriez (1989:279-280).

In reference to issues in designing a query processor, Gardarin and Valduriez discuss several type of algorithms, optimization granularity, optimizing time, statistics, and phases of query processing. These design issues, these scholars say, are common to all query processing algorithms. They, therefore, propose a layering of the different phases of query processing, beginning with a calculus query and ending with the execution of operations to produce results (1989:281). These aspects will be discussed separately, albeit briefly.

According to Gardarin and Valduriez, query processing algorithms can be placed into two sensible categories. The first is exhaustive search, in which all possible strategies are enumerated and evaluated, can allow one to determine the optimal strategy to provide a response to a query, as long as the appropriate timing is utilized. The complexity of this approach is combinatorial in the number of relations. However, it is also cost-effective since the number of relations involved in a query is generally very small (typically between one and five), as compared to the number of relations involved in queries expressed in languages of higher expressive power than relational calculus which can be extremely large. The second type of search is through heuristics. This allows one to restrict the search of the solution space, thereby simplifying the problem. The major heuristics include regrouping common subexpressions to avoid duplication; performing operations that restrict the size of intermediate relations first; ordering binary operations in a manner that minimizes the size of intermediate relations; and choosing the best algorithm, given the existence of several, when performing individual operations (1989:282).

As far as optimization granularity is concerned, Gardarin and Valduriez state that most query processing algorithms optimize one query at a time.

This is because, according to them, the problem is already sufficiently complex. This approach, they note, precludes repeated usage of intermediate results from one query to another. By optimizing multiple queries at a time, one can employ the results of one query in processing others and ordering them in such a manner that throughput (number of queries per second) can be maximized. The decision space, however, is so large that its cost of optimization becomes prohibitive (1989:282).

For optimizing timing, Gardarin and Valduriez suggest that the time at which the query is optimized is critical for system performance. They describe three characteristics of query optimization as follows (1989:282- 283):

(1) *Static optimization*, used in commercial systems, is done before execution of the query. It can be viewed as a compilation approach. Because it is difficult to determine precisely the size of intermediate results, static algorithms rely heavily on the accuracy of statistics and estimation formulas. Inaccurate statistics increase error propagation. The main advantage of the static approach is that query optimization, an expensive process, is done once for many executions of the same query. This is particularly important when database queries are embedded in applications programs. However the compilation into low-level access plans exploits the physical database structure. Any change to the database structure invalidates the access plans and requires recompilation. In practice, reorganization (dropping or adding indexes) is rare because it is expensive.

(2) *Dynamic optimization* is done at run time. It can be viewed as an interpretation approach. The main advantage is that it provides exact information on the sizes of intermediate results. Coupled with the exhaustive search of the decision space at each step,

dynamic optimization can determine the optimal strategy. Its main shortcoming is that optimization cannot be amortized over multiple executions of a repetitive query.

(3) Some *hybrid strategies* have been proposed to combine the advantages of both (i.e. static and dynamic) approaches. The query is compiled using a static algorithm, but it can be partially optimized at run time if estimates of intermediate results appear to be incorrect. Although more complex, this approach, used in some commercial systems, is probably best.

As it relates to statistics, Gardarin and Valduriez maintain that static optimization techniques rely on accurate statistics on the database to estimate the size of intermediate results generated by operations on base relations. The trade-off between accuracy of the statistics and their maintenance cost is a direct one. While sophisticated statistics are more precise, they are, nonetheless, expensive to maintain. Statistics that apply to each relation and some important attributes in relations are primarily employed. Typically, relation statistics are relation cardinality, size of tuple, and at certain times proportion of tuples in one relation participating in the join with another relation. Attribute statistics serve as cardinality of the domain (number of possible distinct values) and actual number of distinct values. Two strong assumptions (independence between different attribute values and uniform distribution of attribute values within their domain) are traditionally made in simplifying the use of these statistics in estimating intermediate results (1989:283).

In reference to phases of query processing, Gardarin and Valduriez point out that the problem of query processing can be decomposed into several subproblems reflecting various layers. Since decisions made for one subproblem may affect those made for another, the problems are not independent. To facilitate tractability, the subproblems are generally treated independently in a top-down manner. Gardarin and Valduriez also state that three main phases are involved when mapping the query into an optimized sequence of operations and to execute them to produce the result: (1) decomposition, which takes place at compile time, decomposes the calculus query using the conceptual schema into a query expressed in relational algebra; (2) optimization, which also takes place at compile time, consists of finding an optimal or quasi-optimal ordering of the relational operations and choosing the access paths to the data, as well as the algorithms for performing database operations; and (3) execution, which takes place at run time, optimizes query generally expressed in a low-level implementation of relational algebra and stored in an execution plan: i.e. an optimized program of low-level database operations akin to a query (1989:283-284).

For query decomposition, Gardarin and Valduriez suggest four steps into which it can be divided: (1) normalization, (2) semantic analysis, (3) simplification, and (4) algebraic restructuring methods. These functions are discussed separately to show how each of them is necessary to simplify an end-user query expressed in relational calculus into a query expressed in relational algebra on the conceptual schema (1989:285).

Beginning with normalization, Gardarin and Valduriez mention that the input query in relational calculus is first lexically, syntactically, and semantically analyzed. After that, it is transformed into a normalized form suitable for further optimization. Lexical and syntactic analysis is akin to those of programming languages. The validity of the query is checked relative to the query language's grammar. The attributes and relations involved in the query are checked to insure their presence in the schema. Also done are type checking of the query qualification and the result specification. The query is rewritten in a normalized form if it is correct up to this point. Most relational calculus languages like SQL make it mandatory for the query to be expressed in *prenex form*—i.e. query where a quantifier-free qualification comes before all qualifications. The query qualification can be transformed into two normal forms: one gives priority to the

ANDs; the other gives priority to the ORs. While the AND predicates are mapped into join or restriction operations, the OR predicates are mapped into union operations. Using the conjunctive normal form calls for doing unions first. And using disjunctive normal form makes it possible to consider the query as independent subqueries (to be discussed later) by unions (1989:285-286).

In the case of semantic analysis, Gardarin and Valduriez say that the objective is to refute incorrect queries. A query that is incorrectly formulated or contradictory is an incorrect one. If disjoint components of the query are useless, then it is incorrectly formulated. This occurs frequently when some join specifications are absent. If its qualification cannot be satisfied by any tuple, a query is contradictory. Algorithms to determine the correctness of a query exist only for a subset of relational calculus, and all of them employ various types of graphs. The two types of graphs that are frequently utilized are (1989:286-287:

(1) *Relational connection graph*—Graph where each node represents a base relation, where an edge between two nodes represents a join, and where an edge going to its source node represents a restriction. A node is added to represent the resulting relation (if any).

(2) *Attribute connection graph*—Graph in which a node is associated to each reference of an attribute or of a constant, where a join is depicted by an edge between the participating attributes, and where a restriction is represented by an edge between an attribute and a constant.

As it pertains to simplification, Gardarin and Valduriez suggest that in relational calculus, different semantically equivalent expressions exist for a given query. If two query expressions yield the same result for any database state, they are said to be equivalent—i.e. queries that produce the same effect for every possible state of the database. Since some expressions are simpler and, therefore, suitable for better performance, they are preferred. To simplify the query expressions, transformation rules can be utilized. Three types of simplification are characterized as follows (1989:289-290):

(1) Elimination of redundancy—A query qualification may contain redundant predicates. The execution of queries with redundant qualifications leads to duplicated work. Queries submitted to the query processor may contain redundant predicates because they generally result from a first translation of user queries by applying view, protection, and semantic integrity rules. Queries resulting from this translation may be unnecessarily redundant and can be simplified. A first (and good) optimization is to eliminate this redundancy by applying well-known idempotency rules of Boolean algebra.

(2) Transitivity—A query qualification may be transformed into an equivalent query qualification by applying the transitive closure of the normalized attribute connection graph. All subgraphs having the same transitive closure lead to equivalent qualifications. It is then possible to retain only the subgraphs that give qualifications that can be more efficiently processed.

(3) Integrity—Semantic integrity rules can be useful to simplify queries. Semantic integrity rules are assertions on all database states. If a query contradicts an integrity assertion, then its answer is void and the database need not be accessed.

As far as algebraic restructuring methods are concerned, Gardarin and Valduriez suggest that one can map a query expressed in relational calculus into a relational algebra program that provides a sequence of relational operations. A simple way to map is to translate every predicate of the qualification into the corresponding relational operation (e.g., join, selection) in the manner in which they appear and then translate the target statement (e.g., SELECT in SQL) of the query into the corresponding operation (e.g., projection). For program manipulation, a graphical representation of a relational algebra can be quite useful. And a relational algebra program can be described by a *relational algebra tree*—i.e. a "tree describing a query where a leaf represents a base relation, an internal node represents an intermediate relation obtained by applying a relational operation, and the root represents the result of the query. The data flow is directed from the leaves to the root" (1989:291).

Gardarin and Valduriez further assert that different queries may be equivalent when expressed in relational calculus. In a similar vein, different relational algebra trees may be equivalent. Some trees may provide much better performance than others because relational operations possess different complexity. The ordering of relational operations and the sizes of the generated intermediate relations are vital factors for optimization. Transformational rules can then be utilized to restructure relational algebra trees. The basic relational algebra operations include Cartesian product, difference, join, projection, restriction, and union. The more complicated ones include grouping or transitive closure and semijoin. All eight rules allow one to do substantial transformations that can optimize query execution. They make it possible to separate unary operations, to group unary operations on the same relation, to effect the commutation of unary operations with binary operations, and to order the binary operations. They also can be applied by a simple restructuring algorithm that employs heuristics that are independent of statistics and physical information on the database (1989:291-292).

Vis-a-vis query optimization, Gardarin and Valduriez discuss processing tress, cost estimation of processing trees, the reduction approach, the exhaustive search approach, and the efficient optimization approach. These aspects serve an important phase of query processing, as they are necessary for selecting a processing strategy that optimizes a given cost function. The input for this optimization phase is an algebraic query involving conceptual relations, and the output is an execution plan of the query. The responsibilities of this phase include making decisions regarding the ordering of database operations, accessing paths to the data, generating algorithms for performing database operations, and delineating intermediate relations to be materialized. Physical database schema and statistics about the database determine the decisions to be undertaken. The processing tree, which may be envisioned as a detailed algebraic tree, can capture a set of decisions that lead to an execution plan. To choose the "optimal" tree, an accurate estimation of the cost of processing trees is imperative. The cost must be predicated upon statistical information about base data and formulae for generating the size of intermediate relations (1989:295-296).

In terms of processing trees, Gardarin and Valduriez posit that an algebraic query expressed in conceptual schema is produced during the decomposition phase of query processing. In the optimization phase that follows, an access plan for the query based on the physical schema is generated by selecting the optimal execution strategy. Included in the conceptual-physical translation is the mapping of relations into physical ones, which are stored in files, and the mapping of algebra operations to primitive datbse operations, which are directly implemented. Based on the assumption that the n-ary storage model exists, then the conceptual- physical mapping relations become trivial as a relation is stored in a single file. Efficiency conditions prevent relational datbse systems from implementing directly relational algebra operations that remain conceptual. Instead, they will support basic operations that limit the access to relations. For example, by accessing the operand relation only once, selection projection without duplicate elimination can be performed directly, as opposed to two successive operations with pure relational algebra. And accroding to Gardarin and Valduriez, the following basic database operations are generally directly supported (1989:296):

* Restriction-projection without duplicate elimination, called *selection*.
* Duplicate elimination.
* Join-project without duplicate elimination, called *join*.
* Set operations (Cartesian product, union, difference, intersections).
* Update operations (insert, delete, modify).

Gardarin and Valduriez also suggest the following basic operations as always being included for mapping non-relational algebra operations (1989:296):

* Sorting.
* Aggregate functions.

And each basic operation, Gardarin and Valduriez add, can be implemented by several algorithms, each optimal under certain conditions (1989:296).

These scholars further point out that the choice of algorithms for performing basic operations, and the ordering of these operations, is dictated by a query execution strategy. They also suggest the following *processing trees* as useful techniques to model particular execution strategies (1989:297-298):

(1) Processing tree (PT)—Tree modeling an execution strategy where a leaf is a base relation and a nonleaf node is an intermediate relation materialized by applying a basic operation algorithm.

(2) Join processing tree (JPT)—Processing tree where the only basic operations considered are joins.

(3)   Binary JPT—JPT where each join has exactly two operand relations.

(4)   Pipelined JPT—JPT where a join can have an arbitrary number of operand relations.

Thus, Gardarin and Valduriez suggest that, by finding the PT of minimal cost, the optimization problem can be formulated. If optimization takes place at run time, then the PT can be dynamically generated. In this case, the exact size of operands, since these are either base relations or intermediate relations materialized at the time of decisions, can be used to estimate the cost. In the case where optimization timing is static, as the final PT must be derived before execution, estimation of the size of intermediate relations becomes paramount for delineating the cost of a PT (1989:298).

On the issue of the cost estimation of processing trees, Gardarin and Valduriez maintain that it is imperative to compute the sum of the costs of the individual basic operations in a PT. CPU time and disk IO time typically comprise the cost measure of a PT. Sometimes, the CPU time is ignored, and the cost measure is approximated by the number of disk accesses. An individual operation's cost with a specific algorithm is itself a monotonic function of the operand relations' cardinalities. In a case where the operand relations are intermediate ones, their cardinalities were also estimated. Consequently two numbers must be predicated for each operand of a PT. These are the individual cost of the operation and the cardinality of its result, with the exception of the final result of the query. Query optimization cannot be achieved without the accurate prediction of the two numbers. Thus, it is imperative for the system to know the cost function of each algorithm that implements a basic operation. And statistical data regarding the physical relations and formulae that predict the cardinality of the result of each operation type call for the estimation of the cardinality of intermediate results. The minimum statistics, according to Gardarin and Valduriez, are the following (1989:298-299):

* The cardinality of the domain of each attribute, *A*, denoted by *dom(A)*.
* The number of distinct values actually present for each attribute, *A*, denoted by *ndist(A)*.
* The minimum and maximum values of each numerical attribute.
* The cardinality of each relation, *R*, denoted by *card(R)*.

These scholars then define the *selectivity factor of a condition*, such as selection of join predicate, as a "proportion of tuples in the database that satisfy the condition" (1989:299).

The cardinality of the result of an operand based on a condition, either selection or join, suggest Gardarin and Valduriez, is a function of the cardinality of the operand relations(s) and the selectivity factor of the condition, represented by *s*. While the cardinality of the result of a selection operation on relation *R* is *s* * *card(R)*, that of the join of two relations *R* and *S* is *s* * *card(R)* * *card(S)*. Indeed, as these authors point out, the accurate estimation of selectivity factors is difficult. This is mainly due to the fact that the traditional simplifying assumptions made by query processors are that (a) attribute values are uniformly distributed within their domain, and (b) attributes are independent. These assumptions are both quite strong and quite often incorrect in the real world. Nonetheless, they allow for simple estimations for selection operations (1989:299).

In addition, Gardarin and Valduriez point out that detailed statistical data are required to generate more accurate estimations of selectivity factors for selection predicates. This will make it possible to relax the assumptions of uniform distribution of attribute values. Histograms and distribution steps are some of these statistics. In general, the estimation of the selectivity factor of the join operation is impractical. Certain systems use the upper-bound value of 1, which is like equating a join to a Cartesian product. This approach is wrong. There is, nonetheless, a frequent case of join where the join selectivity factor can be simply computed. This particular case involves an equi-join based on the key of one relation, say *R1*, and the foreign key of another one, say *R2*. The join selectivity can then be approximated as 1/card*(R2)*—an upper-bound, assuming that each tuple of *R1* participates in the join. The estimation of the cardinalities of the result of other operations is often restricted to upper bounds, because it is easy to compute them. While duplicate elimination, which can reduce significantly the cardinality of an operand relation, is interesting, it is, nevertheless, difficult (1989:300).

As for the reduction approach, Gardarin and Valduriez state that it dynamically generates and executes the query processing tree. A key feature of this technique is that all kinds of JPTs can be generated. The reduction approach has been implemented in INGRES (Interactive Graphics and Retrieval System), and it uses simple heuristics in choosing the first operations and takes into consideration the actual size of the intermediate results to order the subsequent operations. When it comes to evaluating the execution plans, this algorithm does not need to manage statistical data. Its input is a calculus query. Consequently, one must combine the decomposition and optimization phases. First, the reduction algorithm executes the unary, or monovariable, operations; next, it attempts to minimize the sizes of intermediate results in ordering binary operations (1989:300-301).

The basic assumption of the reduction algorithm, according to Gardarin and Valduriez, is that the cost of an operation must be proportional to the size of the operand relations. Essentially, "the reduction algorithm replaces an *N* relation query *Q* by a series of queries *Q1 Q2 ... QN*, where each query *Qi* uses the result of the query *Qi* - 1. It is mainly based on two query transformation techniques, *detachment* and *substitution*" (1989:301).

Gardarin and Valduriez define *detachment* as a "transformation that divides a query into two subqueries, each having a single common relation." They also suggest that, with a detachment, a query Q may be decomposed into two successive queries Q' and Q'', each having only a single, common relation, which is the result of Q'. This detachment facilitates the appearance of simpler operations. The only operations that can be detached are selections and semijoins. Since they are monorelation, selections are easily recognized. By looking at the relation connection graph of a query, semijoins can be isolated. An arc that divides a query into two disjoin graphs makes it possible for a query processor to decompose the query into two subqueries linked by a semijoin. Indeed, not every query can be decomposed by detachment. When a query cannot be detached, it is referred to as being *irreducible*. Semijoins are irreducible and, a fortiori, joins are irreducible. Cyclic queries also are irreducible. Queries that are irreducible are converted into monorelation queries by *tuple substitution*: i.e. "Transformation of an N relation query Q in a set of queries of $(N-1)$ relations by replacing one relation by its actual tuples." The recursive application of tuple substitution until the chain of all queries is monorelation, add Gardarin and Valduriez, can be perceived in terms of a nested-loop solution (1989:301).

In sum, the advantages of the reduction technique are several. They include: (a) simplicity, as it does not require statistics to be maintained about the database; (b) dynamism, as the ordering of joins based on exact cardinalities of relations reduces the probability of generating a bad execution of a query. The shortcomings are (a) the systematic execution of selections before joins could lead to low performance; (b) decomposition and optimization, two expensive tasks that require access to schema data, are conducted at run time and must be repeated for every execution of the same query (Gardarin and Valduriez 1989:303).

As it pertains to the exhaustive search approach, Gardarin and Valduriez assert that it is a very popular technique because of its cost-effectiveness. First developed in System R, the exhaustive search approach performs static optimization based on statistical data. This algorithm's originality hinges on three factors. First, it takes into account IO cost, CPU cost, and existing access paths. Second, since it can have a dramatic effect on performance, it does not apply systematically the heuristic that pushes all selections down the tree. Finally, It takes into account the ordering of the result tuples produced by an execution plan. Both index selectivity and access path properties are taken into account when calculating cost. To assign a selectivity factor to each of the disjunctions of predicates of a query, statistics regarding relations, attributes, and indices are employed. The cardinality of a query's result is derived by the product of the selectivity factors vis-a-vis the cardinalities of the relations. In essence, the exhaustive search approach can be perceived as searching for the best strategy among all possible strategies. Permutation of the join ordering provides the possible strategies for executing a query. And because of its cost-effectiveness, the exhaustive search technique is utilized in many commercial systems (1989:303-306).

In discussing the efficient optimization approach, Gardarin and Valduriez suggest that the objective is to perform static optimization at compile time. Although the time complexity of this algorithm is appealing, its performance sacrifices generality. The linearity of the cost function (*g* function) and the heuristics of handling cyclic queries are the algorithm's two major shortcomings. Indeed, such limitations are not present in the reduction and exhaustive search techniques (1989:306-307).

Finally, for implementation of relational operations, Gardarin and Valduriez investigate the execution of selections and the execution of joins. These aspects of query processing, these authors say, are critical because they represent the primitive operations of a relational system. For execution of selections, the clustering of data in a file is generally done in a way that optimizes the selection operation. The presence of indices on the attributes involved in restriction predicates is contingent upon the efficiency of the selection operation. Nonetheless, there are situations in which indices are useless. An instance is when the selection has bad selectivity. Access of tuples through indices would incur more IOs than scanning sequentially the pages that contain the tuples. Moreover, the file that contains the selected relation may be sequential. Therefore, Gardarin and Valduriez identify two algorithms for performing selection and describe them as follows (1989:308):

(1) Selection without index—Sequential scanning requires that every tuple of the operand relation be compared with the selection qualification. If the qualification is true, then the useful attributes are kept in an intermediate relation. This method implements restriction and projection (without duplicate elimination). Filter processors have been proposed to accomplish such an operation as the data are read either from the disk or main memory.

(2) Selection with index—We now consider the case where indexes on selection attributes are useful. We keep the presentation independent of the index implementation. The only assumption is that an index associates attribute values with addresses (logical or physical), which we will refer to as tuple identifiers (TIDs).

As with selection, Gardarin and Valduriez propose that a distinction can be made between two types of algorithms, given the presence of indices on the join attribute. They then discuss the principles of two basic join algorithms: (1) join without index—in the absence of an index on join attribute, the nested loop method, the sort-merge method, the hashed method, and the semijoin method are employed; (2) join with index—in this case, the join algorithms of the presence of an index on join attribute of one relation, indices on join attributes of the two relations, and join index are used (1989:309-310).

Indeed, given the preceding discussion, languages for queries and update must be integral components of an economic development relational model. Thus, updates can be treated as functions from the set of database states to itself, and queries as functions from the set of states to the space of relations over all possible schemes. To allow for composition, all operators included in the family of operators of *relational algebra* produce relations as results. Some of these operators are discussed in the following pages.

The *selection* operator refers to a unary operator on relations, defined in terms of propositional formulae. A propositional formula over X can be perceived as a function that associates a Boolean value with each tuple (Atzeni and De Antonellis 1993:13). Figure 6 displays an example of selection on the *project coordinator* relation in Figure 1.

NumberServed > 3m (projectcoordinator)

Coordinator	ProjectCode	NumberServed
Eeee	01	4m
Hhhh	04	4m

Figure 6: A selection

The *projection* operator is in some sense orthogonal to selection: the former considers all tuples of the operand on a subset of the attributes, whereas the latter considers a subset of the tuples of the operand on all the attributes. Therefore, by means of projections, *vertical decompositions* are performed; whereas by means of selection, *horizontal decompositions* are performed. Figure 7 shows an example of projection on the *project coordinator* relation in Figure 1.

ProjectCode, NumberServed (projectcoordinator)

ProjectCode	NumberServed
01	4m
02	2m
03	3m
04	4m

Figure 7: A projection

The *natural join* is when neither relation contains dangling tuples. When the tuple does not contribute to the join, it is said to be *dangling*.

> **Example 9:** The join of the relations *development project* and *project coordinator* are shown in Figure 8. Clearly, the tuples in both relations are joined by project code.

Expressions with unrestricted depth are obtained because all the operators produce relations as their results, and thus it is possible to compose their applications (provided that the intermediate results reflect the definitions of the operators applied to them). Employing again the relations in Figure 1, the following is an example of an expression (its results are shown in Figure 9):

ProjectCode, ProjectType (PROJECTCOORDINATOR fi F
NumberServed > 3m
(PROJECTCOORDINATOR))

Development project fi project coordinator

Projec tCode	Projec tDirec tor	Projec t Type	Expen- diture	Coordi -nator	Number Served
01	Aaaa	Nutri- tion	$8m	Eeee	4m
02	Bbbb	Educa- tion	$10m	Ffff	2m
03	Cccc	Health	$8m	Gggg	3m
04	Dddd	Shelte r	$10m	Hhhh	4m

Figure 8: A natural join

ProjectCode, ProjectType (PROJECTCOORDINATOR fi F
NumberServed > 3m
(PROJECTCOORDINATOR))

ProjectType	Coordinator
Nutrition	Eeee
Shelter	Hhhh

Figure 9: The result of an expression

Expressions involving join and projection are the most typical relational operators. A number of interesting properties may be stated about expressions that involve them, as Atzeni and De Antonellis demonstrate (1993:18-19):

(1) The join operator is commutative and associative. For every r_1, r_2, r_3, it is the case that

$$.r_1 \text{ fi } r_2 = r_2 \text{ fi } r_1$$
$$.(r_1 \text{ fi } r_2) \text{ fi } r_3 = r_1 \text{ fi } (r_2 \text{ fi } r_3)$$

It is therefore possible to write sequences of joins without parentheses,

$$r_1 \text{ fi } r_2 \text{ fi...fi } r_m$$

(2) Projection is a sort of inverse of join, and vice versa.

(3) The operator that joins *m* relations and then projects the result over the schemes of the operands produces a set of *m* relations, each of which is contained in the corresponding operand.

(4) An operator is *idempotent* if it is applied several times, then the result is the same as that of a single application.

(5) Somehow, dual results hold for expressions that perform projections and then rejoin the intermediate results.

(6) There is also a dual notion to that of a complete join.

Furthermore, Yang introduces several query languages and relational database manangement systems. This scholar's discussion of these languages and systems is briefly presented as follows (1986:183-242):

(1) *ISBL and PRTV*—ISBL (Information System Base Language) is an algebraic-based language and is used in an experimental interactive DBMS called PRTV (Pertree Relational Test Vehicle).

(2) *QUEL and INGRES*—QUEL (QUEry) Language is a query language that is supported by a relational database management system called INGRES (Interactive Graphics and Retrieval System). QUEL enables the user to be isolated from the implementations of data, storage structures, access methods, and the operations of algorithms on stored data. QUEL also provides a considerable degree of data independence.

(3) *EQUEL*—Embedded QUEL provides the flexibility of the general purpose programming language C, in addition to the database facilities of QUEL. EQUEL consists of a library and a precompiler. The run-time support library contains all the routines necessary for loading an EQUEL program to provide an interface between C and INGRES. The precompiler converts an EQUEL program into a valid C program with QUEL statements converted to appropriate C code and call to INGRES. The resulting C program is then compiled by the standard C compiler, producing and executable module.

(4) *Query-By-Example and QBE DBMS*—Query-By-Example (abbreviated as QBE) is a query language based on the domain calculus. To use QBE and its DBMS, the user must be authorized.

(5) *PROLOG and PROLOG DBMS*—PROLOG (PROgramming in LOGic) is a higher-level programming language, based on the clausal form of logic. It has been used for applications of symbolic computation in many areas, such as mathematical logic, artificial intelligence, and relational databases. The PROLOG DBMS matches tuples and pushes them onto a stack. The interpreter reads

the top element of the stack. Whenever the interpreter backtracks to obtain another tuple, it pops the top element from the stack.

Flat and Nested Relations

From Cacace and Lamperti, one learns that a *nested flat relation* is a relation that can be derived from a flat relation using a sequence of nest operations (1996:145). And according to Atzeni and De Antonellis, the value of every attribute in every tuple is *atomic*: i.e. it is unique and indivisible (in the database). An attribute whose domain contains only atomic values is called *simple*. An attribute is *multivalued* if its possible values are sets (of values); in this case, the domain is a set of subsets of a given set. An attribute is *structured* if its possible values are tuples (of values); in this instance, the domain is already a relation—and this is not illegal, since a relation is a set (1993:21).

In addition, Atzeni and De Antonellis point out that domains may even have more complex structures, built up from repeated set and tuple constructions. A relation scheme R(X) is in *first normal form* (1NF), or *flat*, if every attribute in X is simple. Otherwise, it is *nested*. In the relational model, only relations in 1NF are considered, in order to provide a simple and uniform way of representing data (1993:21-22).

Relations in Boyce-Codd Normal Form

According to Date and Darwen, *normal forms* can be perceived as "good" ways to structure relations in a relational database. Following E. F. Codd, Date and Darwen explain "good" here to mean that certain redundancies, and thereby certain anomalies in update behavior, do not occur. There exist several levels of normalization. The higher the level, i.e. the higher the normal form, the more desirable it is, generally. *Normalization* for Date and Darwen, therefore, is a process by which a given relation schema is replaced by a set of relation schemes in a higher normal form (1992:448).

And as Date and Darwen recount, the first three normal forms—1NF, 2NF, and 3NF—were first introduced and defined in 1972 by E. F. Codd in a landmark essay. However, the definition of 3NF in the essay suffered from a minor problem: i.e. a relation can be in 3NF and yet still suffer from certain redundancies of the kind that Codd was trying to exclude by his definitions. In his attempt to remedy this shortcoming, Raymond F. Boyce in 1973 defined a new normal form which he referred to, logically enough, as fourth normal form (4NF). Boyce's definition was subsequently refined by both Boyce and Codd, and the refined version was published in a joint paper in 1974. The following is a simplified, but accurate, version of the refined definition, as stated by Date and Darwen (1992:438):

> A relation R is in [the new normal form] if the only functional dependencies in R are of the form K X, where K is a candidate key of R and X is some column of R.

Intuitively, add Date and Darwen, the preceding definition proffers the notion that only functional dependencies in the relation are those that are implied by the candidate keys of the relation. They also note that the expression "K X" can be read as "X is functionally dependent on K," or "K functionally determines X" (1992:438). Furthermore, Date and Darwen posit that a relation schema is in *Boyce-Codd normal form* if whenever X Y is a nontrivial *functional dependency* (FD) of the schema, necessarily X is a superkey. A relatively more technical discussion of Boyce-Codd normal form can be found in Yang (1986:169-179).

Date and Darwen also show that, if a relation schema is in Boyce-Codd normal form and some key is simple, then it is in fourth normal form; however, it does not necessarily mean that the relation schema is in projection-join normal form. These results facilitate easy comprehension and are sufficient to guarantee the higher normal forms. Thus, they provide a practical database design guideline that may reduce the difficulty of the database designer. They also ease the task of the database instructor, who must provide students with practical situations in which projection-join normal form (PJ/NF) can be derived without requiring knowledge of multivalued and join dependencies (1992:448).

In addition, as Atzeni and De Antonellis point out, *relations in Boyce-Codd normal form* deal with the following three types of anomalies (1993:24-25):

(1) *Update anomalies* are those related to redundancy.

(2) *Insertion anomalies*—it is not possible to insert an item of a kind if the inventory number if that item is not known.

(3) *Selection anomalies*—the elimination of all the individuals of one kind of an item leads to the loss of information on the item of that particular kind.

Atzeni and De Antonellis add that, more generally, the occurrence of anomalies is due to the presence, in a single relation, of different concepts. The study of problems related to the elimination of anomalies leads to the definition of *normal forms* for relation schemes, which are expressed in terms of integrity constraints that formalize properties of the application (e.g., in the preceding examples, each project has a unique project direc-tor). The fundamental normal; forms refer to a constraint called *functional dependency*, which corresponds to an integrity constraint on the relation scheme; thus, it constitutes the assertion of a property that must be valid for all possible instances of a relation scheme (1993:25-26).

Conclusion

This chapter clearly demonstrates that a relational model of data can help to insure project accountability in African countries, because it can facilitate data independence. This will allow computer programmers the ability to overcome the limitations of hierarchical and network models. This chapter also provides the computer science student with some useful information on normal form, keys, basic operators for relational algebra, and the major role played by query languages in the theory and practice of relational databases.

Chapter 7

Epilogue: A Call for a Public Choice Approach

This chapter seeks to offer an alternative approach to insure sustainable economic development in African countries. It begins by first examining various development approaches that have been employed on the African continent since its independence explosion in the 1960s and the reasons for their failures. In lieu of the results of these models, a **Public Choice** approach, when buttressed by a series of computer models, is suggested in this book as an alternative to insure project accountability for sustainable economic development in African states. The underlying presuppositions of the present chapter are: (1) if self-interest is a powerful motivator in the marketplace, there is every reason to believe that it will also be a motivating factor when choices are made collectively to promote economic development; (2) if market choices are influenced by changes in projected personal costs relative to benefits, there is every reason to expect that such changes will also influence political choices for economic development. Thus, the essence of this chapter hinges upon its attempt to create a fusion between the disciplines of Computer Science and Economics.

Perhaps the following simple anecdote will serve to illustrate the need for an alternative approach to insure project accountability to spur economic development in Africa:

During a recent professional meeting, a notable African scholar presented his paper on "Theory of De-development." At the conclusion of his presentation, a member of the audience, who had traveled all the way from Kenya to attend the Conference, remarked: "Enough of the theorizing! We need practical answers to make sure that anyone who drives on a straight course on most African roads is not driving drunk. For a sober person would have to drive zigzag to escape the massive manholes (that is, potholes) on those roads."

As the preceding excerpt suggests, scholars investigating the issue of economic development in Africa must 'explain' a definable range of solutions by showing how it coheres with such areas, allows us to predict them, and may lead either to comprehension, control, or both. If our pursuits remain overwhelmingly abstract, we may be searching for the elusive prescriptions for economic development in areas where there is inadequate light for us to conduct the search.

The economics literature offers a variety of models showing the path toward insuring project accountability to spur economic development. Yet, when a developing country pleads for specific answers, these economists can refer to only partial solutions or states of development nature so theoretical and abstract that few have ever really been tested.

Since its independence explosion in the 1960s, Africa has witnessed a variety of economic development approaches. These approaches include the simple growth model, the redistribution with growth model, the import- substitution model, the socialist model, the national self-reliance model, and the regional integration or collective self-reliance model (see discussion of these models on the following pages). More than thirty-five years after the independence explosion, the performance of many African economies remains to be desired. Of the twenty-five poorest countries in the world, eighteen of them are in Sub-Saharan Africa. Over the last decade, the economic performance of these countries has declined. Food production has declined by over twenty percent. Between 1980 and 1990, the average annual growth in per capita Gross National Product (GNP) was between one percent and a negative one-tenth of a percent (see various World Banks reports).

The present chapter seeks, therefore, to offer an alternative approach, **Public Choice**, when buttressed by a relational model of data, as a relatively more viable path toward sustainable economic development in Africa. The Public Choice approach has significantly advanced our understanding of the collective decision-making process in recent years. Public Choice applies the principles and methodology of economics to collective choices. Public Choice theory postulates that individual behavior in the political arena will be motivated by considerations similar to those that influence market behavior. If self-interest is a powerful motivator in the marketplace, there is every reason to believe that it will also be a motivating factor when choices are made collectively to promote economic development. If market choices are influenced by changes in projected personal costs relative to benefits, there is every reason to expect that such changes will also influence political choices for economic development. Public Choice theory, in essence, advances the view that the number of saints and sinners in both the economic and public sectors will be comparable.

By analyzing the behavior of people in the marketplace within an economic development perspective, one can develop a logically consistent theory of behavior that can be tested against reality. Through theory and empirical testing, the analyst can seek to explain various economic development actions of decision-makers and, in general, how the market operates.

Thus, the current chapter examines the following issues: (1) previous development models utilized in Africa and the reasons for their foibles, and (2) Public Choice, couched within the prisms of a relational model of data, as an alternative model. These aspects can guide the rational decision- maker toward avoiding the shortsightedness effect which has hampered many African economies over the years. That is, the misallocation of resources that results because public sector action is biased: (a) in favor of proposals yielding clearly defined current benefits in exchange for difficult- to-identify future costs, and (b) against proposals with clearly identifiable current costs yielding less concrete and less obvious future benefits.

Previous Development Models Utilized in Africa and Reasons for Their Failures

When the independence explosion took place on the African continent in the 1960s, a majority of the countries had very close economic ties with their former colonial masters. Particularly in the case of the francophone countries, the ties were much stronger: France, for example, accounted for three-quarters of the external trade of Benin, Chad, Niger and Senegal at independence. Because most African countries had given preferential tariff treatment to imports from the metropole during the colonial period, their currencies were similarly tied to those of the metropole. The colonial powers had typically monopolized foreign investments and aid donation in the colonies. Decolonization offered African governments the opportunity to diversify their economic links and pursue development strategies that could allow them to reduce their economic dependence on the former colonial masters.

In this section of the present chapter, the development strategies that African governments have pursued since independence and the reasons for their shortcomings are explored. The focus is on the theoretical presuppositions of these development models and the results yielded after their implementation.

The Simple Growth Model

The *simple growth model* can be traced to the "Western" model of development. In the words of Nisbet (1969:7), "developmentalism is one of the oldest and most powerful of all Western ideas." The central idea engendered in this development thinking is the metaphor of *growth*. Thus, development, according to Nisbet, is conceived as being "organic, immanent, directional, cumulative, irreversible, and purposive. Furthermore, it implies structural differentiation and increasing complexity."

The early discussion on modern economic development for poorer countries (that is, the late 1950s and the early 1960s) had an optimistic tone which may be difficult to explain today. This optimism was mainly a manifestation of the dynamic growth experienced by the industrialized countries themselves under the Marshall Plan as a successful demonstration case in development, and also the philosophic tradition in the West which looked upon growth as more or less inevitable. The Keynesian "revolution" in economics had taught Western economists and Africans trained in Western economics that the state sometimes had to give a helping hand, but few doubted that the future of African and other developing countries on the whole was reflected in the experience of the industrialized countries. The simple formula was: just find out the Incremental Capital-Output ratio and the desired rate of growth. Then one can (after due consideration to the rate of population growth) arrive at the appropriate level of investment needed for economic growth (Hettne 1978:11). Foreign capital inflows were seen as a 'pump-priming' mechanism intended to help a developing country's savings and tax receipts as well as investment to rise steadily (Bangura 1995:25).

More sociologically-minded observers stressed the importance of a leading sector (private or public) and the emergence of the entrepreneurial elite as stimuli for economic development. Growth, as expounded by scholars such as Rostow (1960), was thus seen mainly as a function of investment and not too many observers doubted that a process of economic growth through a series of "stages" would in the end benefit an entire country. This explains why the 1960s were heralded the *First Development Decade* in anticipation of the successes that were expected to follow.

During the early 1970s, however, many African and other developing countries began to encounter difficulties in fulfilling the growth development strategy. Even Western economists trained in formal theory began to sense new realities. Adelman and Morris, for example, capture this idea quite well when they state:

> We had shared the prevailing view among economists that economic growth was economically beneficial to most nations. We had also greatly questioned the relevance today of the historical association of successful economic growth with the spread of parliamentary democracy. Our results proved to be at variance with our preconceptions (1973:vii).

It is evident from this excerpt that these observers exemplify a renewed interest in the connection between economic growth and income distribution. The major reason for this emphasis was the visible aspects of the extent of poverty: recurrent starvation, mass unemployment, political unrest, etc. What was taking place in African and other developing countries during the "development decade" was growth with poverty instead of development.

As Legum and his partners (1979:151-160) summarize, based on data from across the African Continent, post-colonial African countries by the mid-1970s had perpetuated or generated staggering income inequalities and had maintained much of their populations in conditions of absolute poverty. These economies, moreover, remained very much toward raw material production and export for previous metropolitan markets (namely France, Britain and Belgium) with some diversification of markets to include other EEC (European Economic Community) member states, especially Germany and the Netherlands. In only eight of the 35 independent African states had a non-EEC country become the major trading partner by the mid-1970s. Also, only in Mauritius were manufactures among the principal products exported.

The Redistribution with Growth Model

The new strategy implied in the *redistribution with growth model* exemplified a modification of, rather than a clear break with the *simple growth model*. First, the analysis retained much of the optimism of the earlier "trickle down" assumptions in asserting that the benefits of growth, empirically, had a tendency to be concentrated in the early stages but that further increase in concentration were by no means inevitable. Second, the social engineering approach to development as Chenery and his partners (1962, 1966a, 1966b, 1966c, 1970, 1974) purported, was still adhered to, in that they believed that to deal with the problems of poverty groups governments need to design overall programs or policy packages rather than a set of isolated projects. This is simply a continuation of the old strategy of "balanced growth" extended to include social development as well (Bangura 1995:27-28).

At center stage of the shortcoming of the redistribution with growth strategy in Africa is the fact that most of the continent's governments could not significantly raise mass living standards by maintaining their reliance on traditional primary production exports; yet, this reliance was maintained. In extreme cases such as Ghana, the government's attempt to increase its reliance on cocoa exports led to a sharp decline in total revenues received because of the price elasticity of demand conditions for the commodity. Prices for most primary products exported from Africa were unstable and remain so to the present day. Such price changes ushered dramatic ups and downs in economic conditions in Africa, leaving the planning of structural change extremely difficult and the avoidance of periodic foreign-exchanges practically impossible (Legum et al. 1979:161-162).

A corollary to this problem was the fact that the purchasing power of most African commodity exports in the global market was declining over much of the post-independence period. Between 1960 and 1972, overall barter terms of trade for developing countries in general declined by an annual average of 0.3 percent. The purchasing power of those countries' exports (excluding petroleum) declined by an annual average of 1.4 percent during the same period. The remarkable upsurge in commodity prices during 1973-1974 was quickly reversed by 1975. African countries were left worse off because of the decline in prices for their commodities and these economies' requirements for high-priced oil imports (Legum et al. 1979:162).

The emergence of new resource exports in the post-independence period provided a few African countries an escape from these strains. Petroleum discoveries and development in Gabon and Nigeria, iron ore in Mauritania, and copper in Botswana provided these countries such escape.

In a few other countries, possibilities for diversification rested on new agricultural products (for example, cashews in Tanzania) and expanded peasant cash cropping (for example, tea and pyrethrum in Kenya). But these primary products production did not provide the rapid income advances intermediary bourgeoisies needed to finance their own embourgeoisement and some significant increase in standards of living. The subsequent outcome, as to be expected, was political instability (Legum et al. 1979:162-163). These developments led many African countries to promote industrialization policies based on import-substitution.

The Import-Substitution Model

The underlying tenet of the *import-substitution model* is that in order to industrialize, developing countries must also decide whether to produce manufactured goods for export or to replace imports because (a) their manufactured imports indicate the existence of a domestic market for particular products, (b) barriers against foreign competition could easily be erected, and (c) the strategy is believed to relieve even greater balance of payments problems later. Import tariffs, which tend to become progressively higher with higher stages of processing, could provide the needed protection.

In their examination of import-substitution industrialization in Africa, Chazan and her colleagues (1988:244-246) state that the continent's experience with this strategy has, on the whole, been a particularly unhappy one. These observers provide a number of reasons for their assertion. These reasons are presented below.

To begin with, instead of conserving scarce foreign exchange, import-substitution industrialization proved to be import-sensitive because many of the capital goods and components used in manufacturing had to be imported. The foreign exchange problem was often exacerbated where import-substitution industrialization was conducted by a subsidiary of the transnational corporation, since its profits, interest, and dividends were repatriated to its parent company overseas. Instead of reducing dependence, the strategy simply led to a change in the nature of that dependence—on foreign technology, for instance.

In addition, import-substitution industrialization led to a misallocation of resources. As infant industries failed to grow up, they continued to be dependent on high levels of protection from potential competitors. With this high level of protection came little incentive for industry to become more efficient. The inevitable consequence was that local consumers were subjugated to unnecessarily high prices. A corollary was that the strategy discriminated directly against other sectors, especially agriculture, which were dependent on inputs from import-substitution industries. The inefficiency of these industries also meant that they could not sell their goods on the world market in order to reap economies of scale.

Other policies associated with import-substitution industrialization also caused certain distortions. In order to reduce the relative cost of inputs needed by industry, governments had to maintain overvalued exchange rates. Export sectors such as agriculture and mining suffered because of this policy as their products became relatively more expensive for foreigners to buy. The state corporations became even more inefficient because governments demanded that they employ secondary-school graduates and provide below-cost services to other sectors of the economies.

Furthermore, a number of serious policy errors were also made, particularly in opting for the latest high-technology processes as opposed to those appropriate for local conditions. An example was the creation of six vehicle assembly plants in Nigeria that were largely dependent on imported materials. The range of models produced was so wide that production runs were quite short. The multiplication of plants also led to very low levels in production capacity. As a consequence, some of the plants recorded a negative value added in manufacturing. The costs of assembly in Nigeria were actually in excess of the cost of importing a fully- built vehicle from abroad. Another example is the large automated bakery in Tanzania which was more capital-intensive than the country's oil refinery. The bakery became so highly dependent on imported wheat that it displaced a number of local, more efficient manufacturers.

In sum, the import-substitution strategy failed to bring about the much anticipated dramatic increase in local manufacturing. The seven percent growth in manufacturing value added in the period 1963-1973 was reduced to 5.7 percent in the period 1973-1981. During this latter period, fourteen African countries actually recorded a decrease in the manufacturing value added. This same period also saw the contribution of manufacturing to total GDP (Gross Domestic Product) fall in twenty Sub-Sahara African countries. By 1983, the continent's share of world manufactured exports had fallen by almost half over the years 1970 to 1976 to a low of 0.6 percent (Chazan et al. 1988:245-246).

The Socialist Model

"African Socialism," asserts Hettne (1978:52), "is a vague concept, to say the least, and encompasses many diverse viewpoints." He discerns five major groups:

(1) *Afro Marxists* emphasized Marxist-Leninist ideas of economic development and political structure and included Ahmed Ben Bella of Algeria, Ahmed Sekou Touré of Guinea, Gamal Abdel Nasser of Egypt, Kwame Nkrumah of Ghana, Modibo Keita of Mali, Mengistu Haile Mariam of Ethiopia, Jose Eduardo dos Santos and Agostinho Neto of Angola, Samora Machel of Mozambique, Mohammed Siad Barre of Somalia, the military leaders of Benin and Madagascar, Luiz De Almeida Cabral and Joao Bernago Vieira of Guinea Bissau.

(2) *Radical Socialists* took a more critical approach and moved toward Marxism. They included leaders in the Congo Brazzaville—at least before the 1977 coup.

(3) *Moderate Socialists* included Jomo Kenyata of Kenya and Kenneth Kaunda of Zambia who favored a state-controlled socialist economy but were at the same time anxious to attract foreign investment capital.

(4) *Social Democrats* were closely connected to European socialism and were frequently pro-Western in outlook. These included

Senegal's Leopold Sedar Senghor and briefly Zaire's Mobutu Sese Seko and Chad's Ngarta Tombalbaye.

(5) *Agrarian Socialist or Populist* was Tanzania's Julius Nyerere and his Ujaama philosophy.

In sum, African Socialism covered a wide ideological spectrum, ranging from Marxist-Leninist to populist ideas very similar to the Russian Narodniks or Gandhi in India. The African founding fathers espoused notions of socialism and shared an aversion to colonialism. They saw independence as the way to build a new and prosperous Africa.

Early African socialists proclaimed a commitment to the creation of egalitarian societies, just, and self-sufficient polity. The state was envisioned as the mechanism through which these objectives could be met. These pioneers extolled political centralization and mobilization as the tools for real economic and social transformations on the African continent (Chazan et al 1988:150).

As a philosophy of rule, however, African Socialism barely survived the first decade of independence. By the early 1970s Nkrumah, Ben Bella, and Keita had been deposed, Nasser had died, and Nyerere and Touré had taken different political paths. Nonetheless, the impact of these first ideological experiments has lasted their purporters. African Socialism as a means of instilling a sense of national pride and African dignity still has widespread appeal on the continent. The commitment to Pan-Africanism is often traced back to these leaders because they were the first to attempt the exposition of a coherent, albeit inconsistent, system of political and economic ideas. Their concepts have emerged as measuring rods for subsequent strategies.

The National Self-Reliance Model

The *national self-reliance model* calls for a conscious policy by developing countries to "de-link" from the global economy. As a concept, self-reliance was inaugurated by the Non-Aligned Countries at their 1970 meeting in Lusaka and was further elaborated at their 1972 foreign ministers conference in Georgetown. It was seen as an antithesis to "dependency." The concept emerged just before the concept NIEO (New International Economic Order), which sought international co-operation as opposed to withdrawal from the global economic system. In essence, national self-reliance did not mean autarky—a complete severance of all economic relations with the outside world, but a partial disengagement of a country from the dominant relationship prevailing in the global economic system.

The theoretical rationale for national self-reliance as a relatively more comprehensive development approach has been summarized by Johan Galtung in thirteen hypotheses (see Hettne 1978:32):

(1) Through SR (self-reliance) priorities will change towards production for basic needs for those most in need.

(2) Through SR mass participation is ensured.

(3) Through SR local factors are utilized much better.

(4) Through SR creativity is stimulated.

(5) Through SR there will be more compatibility with local conditions.

(6) Through SR there will be much more diversity of development.

(7) Through SR there will be less alienation.

(8) Through SR ecological balance will be more easily attained.

(9) Through SR important externalities are internalized or given to neighbors at the same level.

(10) Through SR solidarity with others at the same level gets a solid base.

(11) Through SR ability to withstand manipulation due to trade dependency increases.

(12) Through SR the military defense capability of the country increases.

(13) Through SR as a basic approach today's Center and Periphery are brought on a more equal footing.

As Hettne (1978:32) so aptly points out, this list of advantages of self-reliance appears quite utopian and that Galtung is at pains to point out that the thirteen propositions should be conceived as hypotheses about possible effects. The question here, then, is: How has national self-reliance fared in Africa?

National self-reliance became a prominent concept of the Mobutu government in Zaire in the early 1970s. It was accompanied by the notion of "authenticity"—the Africanization of names. National self-reliance was also emphasized by the Acheampong government in Ghana in 1972-1975. After 1975, it lost its aura on the African continent. It was later revived by the populist regimes in Burkina Faso and Ghana in the mid-1980s. The two countries that have pursued a more consistent national self-reliance policy in Africa are Algeria and Tanzania (Chazan et al.

1988:273). It is hoped that a brief examination of how these two countries have employed national self-reliance will give the reader a sampling of how the strategy has fared in Africa.

Tanzania's commitment to national self-reliance, which is intertwined with a socialist philosophy, can be traced back to the Arusha Declaration authored by Nyerere in February 1967. The declaration began with a frank assessment of Tanzania's economic woes and prospects. Nyerere's major concern was with the extensive demands his citizens were making for government services which were becoming difficult to fulfill, even with substantial foreign economic assistance. Tanzania also learned very quickly just how unreliable foreign aid could be. Relations between Tanzania and its three largest aid donors deteriorated: with West Germany because Tanzania had established diplomatic relations with East Germany; with the United States over accusations that the CIA (Central Intelligence Agency) was attempting to overthrow Nyerere's government; and with Britain because of an inadequate response from the British over the Unilateral Declaration of Independence by the white minority in Rhodesia (now Zimbabwe). West Germany and Britain froze their aid to Tanzania making it impossible for Tanzania to meet its development targets outlined in the First Five-Year Plan it had adopted in 1964 (Chazan et al. 1988:273-274).

With relatively very little aid coming from the former Eastern bloc countries, Tanzania had no choice but to pursue a policy of national self-reliance if it wished to continue its independent foreign policy stance. The Arusha Declaration pointed out that if individuals were self-reliant, then, districts, regions, and the whole country would be self-reliant. Because the vast majority of the Tanzanian population lived in the rural areas, Nyerere placed greater emphasis on rural development by providing those areas with education, health care, and potable water. He reasoned, therefore, that priority in industrialization should be given to industries that could service the needs of the rural population. Greater self-reliance was seen as the way to: (a) necessitate acceptance by the population of (sometimes lower- quality) locally produced goods instead of imported luxuries, (b) reduce imports, and (c) diversify Tanzania's trade links in order to lessen its dependence on existing markets and suppliers (Chazan et al. 1988:274).

Although many Ujaama villages now existed on paper, very few operated on a collective basis as intended. By 1975, the government had backed down from the idea of communal production. The villagization program disrupted agricultural production; a situation further compounded by the 1974 drought. Thus, Tanzania had to import food rather than being self-sufficient in agriculture. This, in turn, meant that Tanzania had to face the major burden of using its scarce resources for foreign exchange. Most discouraging was that very few villagers even had a clear understanding of what self-reliance meant in practice (Chazan et al. 1988:275).

Tanzania's case clearly exemplifies the difficulties weak, dependent economies encounter when they seek to effect significant changes in the global economy. While, on the one hand, Tanzania has been successful in pursuing its foreign policy in the political arena, its economic policy, on the other hand, has been hampered by factors beyond its control and by the structural constraints of the global economy.

Algeria's national self-reliance approach, like that of Tanzania, is intertwined with a socialist development philosophy. Algeria, however, is well endowed with energy resources. It has been able, therefore, to articulate a self-reliance policy that stresses national control over natural resources as the major factor of being "master in one's own house" (Chazan et al. 1988:277).

The major features of Algeria's self-reliance policy include the nationalization of foreign-owned companies, creation of many state-owned enterprises, insistence upon Algerian instead of expatriate managers, reinvestment of energy revenues in order to lessen recourse to foreign capital, and a policy of leadership in the affairs of developing countries, especially in the call for a NIEO. Self-reliance, to the Algerians, means national control (Chazan et al. 1988:277).

The 1976 National Charter, which is the Algerian equivalence to Tanzania's Arusha Declaration, stresses national accumulation of capital for investment as opposed to becoming dependent on foreign investment and urges other developing countries to follow suit. The rationale is that a country has to count first on itself in order to exert influence on the prices of its raw materials (Chazan et al. 1988:278).

However, during the period of concentrated investment in industrialization, Algeria saw its agricultural production decline. With its population rapidly growing, Algeria has become dependent upon food imports (Chazan et al. 1988:278).

As in Tanzania, Algeria's self-reliance program has been struck a serious blow because of its inability to increase its agricultural production. The decline of oil prices in the mid-1980s also forced Algeria to tighten its belt and revise its investment projections. But unlike Tanzania, Algeria is endowed with energy resources which allow it to pursue its goal of becoming the master in its own house.

The Regional Integration or Collective Self-Reliance Model

The presupposition of the *regional integration model* (or *collective self-reliance*, as other writers refer to it) is that to realize greater self-reliance, a country must inevitably depend on the cooperation from other countries that share similar characteristics and goals. African countries learned very quickly after independence that in order for them to overcome the problems of limited economic resources economic cooperation with their neighbors was sensible strategy. What, then, has been the result of regional integration in Africa?

The idea of regional integration in Africa is not new. Before independence, colonial powers instituted regional integration systems for their own needs instead of those of Africans. Transportation networks linking peripheral areas and coastal centers were created by colonial administrators to minimize their financial commitments, coordinate markets, and establish common currency areas under their rule. Britain and France even promoted the formation of federations, common service organizations and common banking systems among their colonies (Legum et al. 1979:177).

Post-independence regional integration in Africa, however, is of a different sort. While international capital favored the creation of free trade areas from which it stood to benefit, it nonetheless sought to undermine those regional integrative systems that through planning might inhibit its freedom of action. Multinational Corporations are particularly reluctant to encourage regional integration if they have medium- or large-size market and some limited local industrial capacity (Legum et al. 1979:177).

African integrative systems are characterized by substantial economic disparities among the member states. As such, a variety of fiscal and planning mechanisms were built into integrative systems to compensate less industrialized African partners for the unequal distribution of gains that generally result from the liberalization of trade. But the failure to implement such schemes heightened conflicts over cost-benefit issues within these integrative systems. In some of the systems (for example, the Organization pour la mise en valeur de la Vallée du Fleuve Sénégal), these conflicts led to the transformation of the associations and their abandonment of planning objectives. In other systems (such as ECOWAS—Economic Community of West African States), cost-benefit conflicts led to many postponements in the signing of the treaties and subsequent delays in implementing key harmonizing elements in them. In still others (such as EAC—East African Community), similar conflicts led to the dissolution of the systems (Legum et al. 1979:178).

SADCC (South African Development Coordination Conference), which grew out of the grouping of Front Line States (Angola, Botswan, Lesotho, Malawi, Mozambique, Tanzania, Swaziland, Zambia, and Zimbabwe), created to promote the transition to majority rule in Zimbabwe, has emerged as the most innovative attempt on the African continent to translate aspirations of regional integration into reality. The system enjoyed moderate success in its first years of existence. It was able to attract finance for a number of projects in the transportation and communications fields. There was an increase in the amount of trade between some of the member states. The trade was often conducted on the basis of barter or paid for in local currencies (Chazan et al. 1988:270-271).

Despite this moderate success, SADCC faced two major vulnerabilities. The first had to do with the fact that the organization is heavily dependent on foreign donors for its projects. Its annual donors' conferences have been able to attract support for some projects, but the total assistance provided has fallen far short of the system's expectations. In a number of cases, the aid had actually represented the redirection of existing pledges instead of additional finance. Aid donors demonstrated a marked reluctance to finance SADCC's agricultural and industrial projects. Reliance on foreign assistance was somewhat paradoxical since the organization's stated goal is to reduce dependence of foreign aid (Chazan et al. 1988:271).

The second source of vulnerability was the Front Line States nemesis: South Africa. Because Pretoria perceived SADCC to be a challenge to its hegemony in the region, it sought to undermine the organization. South Africa frequently invaded those states that share a border with it and also sponsored guerilla movements hostile to the established Front Line governments (such as RENAMO—Mozambique National Resistance Movement and UNITA—National Union for the Total Independence of Angola) to carry out acts of sabotage in these countries—destruction of transportation and communication links, blowing up power lines, etc. Other forms of South Africa's sabotage were quite subtle: refusing to provide railroad locomotive to head trains originating in Zimbabwe; redirecting South Africa's trade away from the port of Maputo; and offering reduced tariffs on rail transport through South Africa for Zimbabwe's main exports of tobacco and cotton to encourage traders not to use SADCC routes (Chazan et al. 1988:272).

The foregoing review of the economic models African Countries have employed since independence clearly indicates that successful policy reforms and economic development in Africa call for substantial political will on the part of African governments. In light of the fact that the international community has failed to provide the requisite external support necessary to promote substantive economic development on the continent, African leaders must shoulder this responsibility by being willing to make the painful policy decisions.

Public Choice as an Alternative Approach

In order to analyze the behavior of people in the marketplace, economists develop a logically consistent theory of behavior that can be tested against reality. Through theory and empirical testing, they attempt to explain various economic actions of decision-makers, and in general, how the market works.

This approach is also plausible in analyzing the behavior of people in the public sphere. To explain how the collective decision-making process actually works, a logically consistent theory linking individual behavior to collective action, an analysis of the implications of the theory, and the testing of these implications against reality are called for.

A number of Public Choice theorists have made great contributions to our understanding of resource allocation by the public sector. (I am referring here to the contributions of Kenneth Arrow, Duncan Black, James Buchanan, Charles Bullock, Anthony Downs, David Mayhew, Norman Nicholson, William Niskanen, Mancur Olson, Clifford Russell, Robert Tollison, and Gordon Tullock; see full citations in the bibliography.)

These social scientists have also provided a number of basic characteristics that influence outcomes in both the market and public sectors. Gwartney and Stroup (1983:71-73) summarize the differences between these two sectors based on these theorists' work. These are examined here in terms of the African context. The first question to be dealt with here, however, is: Why is Public Choice relevant for economic development?

To say that Public Choice is relevant to employing a relational model of data to insure project accountability in facilitating economic development in African states is to say that economic development will require some collective decisions; that those decisions will be made at the national level; and that those participating in the decisions (Africans with whose welfare we are concerned) can be viewed as rational and self-interested actors. It is, of course, impossible to prove that Africans, or any other people from any other continent for that matter, are rational and self-interested actors in the business of life. The issue, however, is not whether all Africans always behave rationally and self-interestedly. It is, rather, what kind of behavior predominates and therefore around which behavior it makes sense to design institutions.

Competitive Behavior in the Market and Public Sectors

Competitive behavior exists in both the market and public sectors. Just as in the market sector where businesses compete for the consumers' money, so must politicians compete for the voters' ballots in the public arena. Ministers and directors of agencies, like their counterparts in the private sector, compete for additional funds, promotions, and additional power. Ethnic groups compete for power and favorable policies. The nature of the competition and the criteria for success do differ between the sectors. However, both sectors must deal with the reality of scarcity. Thus, the need for rationing is evident in both of them. The need to ration scarce resources inevitably leads to competitive behavior.

In the African context, this means that the countries which are still under personal and military rule must adopt democratic rule within what has come to be known as the Schumpeterian framework: that is, the "institutional arrangement for arriving at political decisions in which individuals acquire the power to decide by means of a competitive struggle for the people's vote" (Schumpeter 1950:269).

Of course, the democratic idea is not foreign to the African continent. Morna, in a November 28, 1990 article in *The Chronicle of Higher Education*, for example, cites a book written by a group of academics from Kenya, Tanzania and Uganda entitled *Democratic Theory and Practice in Africa* (1989), in which it is clearly documented that democracy was deeply rooted in African traditions and struggles against colonialism.

Among the Kikuyus, for instance, government was by "committee". There were no formal chiefs. Every man could hope to be elected at least once to direct tribal policy. The tribe was divided into halves, rather like the American two-party system. Each half had its full complement of elders, judges, and parliamentarians throughout the chain of command. While the officials of one half acted, officials of the other side listened and consulted (Vlahos 1967:192-193).

Public Sector Organization and the Individual Consumption-Payment Link

A consumer who wants to obtain a commodity must be willing to give up money for that commodity. There is a one-to-one correspondence between consuming the commodity and paying the price charged in the market. This is not the case, however, in collective action. Governments do not usually establish a one-to-one relationship between the citizen's tax bill and the amount of political goods or services he or she receives.

A citizen's tax bill will be the same whether he or she likes or dislikes the government's spending policies. In some cases, the citizen could be made worse off by a government program and still ends up paying for it.

In African countries, indirect taxes predominate. These indirect taxes include residency taxes, sales taxes, excise taxes, import taxes, and export taxes. Because the economies are not fully monetized and records of financial transactions are rarely kept, direct personal income taxes are difficult to collect. Indirect taxes are generally regressive. The absence of progressive personal tax systems, then, means that taxes are not collected based on a citizen's ability to pay. Consequently, taxation of African farmers is relatively high; levies of 40-50 percent are commonly imposed on export crops. This is in addition to taxation resulting from overvalued exchange rates or inefficient market systems. In the cases of Nigeria, Somalia and Sudan, these countries had not introduced sales taxes up until 1981. In fact, many other African countries generate very modest revenues because of their failure to exploit their tax bases fully (The World Bank 1981:40-41).

Hence, the high level of taxation of export crops through export taxes and marketing board levies have kept export production in many African countries below what they could be. This, in turn, has contributed to the steep decline in Africa's share in the world market.

African countries have to impose less tax burdens on the "motor" sectors of their economies as well as to check expenditures by using fees and charges to a greater degree. A shift toward heavier taxation of tradeables would give African tax systems the ability to increase revenues as outputs increase. Given present African circumstances, a single-stage ad valorem sales tax collected at the point of local manufacture is relatively more suitable.

Indeed, taxation may raise prices, but it is from the economic point of view superior to inflation as a source of finance for capital formation because (a) the effect of taxation on prices is likely to be much smaller, (b) the discipline of controlling the money supply is easier to maintain, and (c) the incidence of taxation can be controlled more fairly and efficiently.

Scarcity and Aggregate Consumption-Payment Link in the Market and Public Sectors

The reality of the aggregate consumption-aggregate payment link will persist despite a government's ability to break the link between payment for a good and the right of the individual to consume that good. In order to provide scarce goods, certain alternatives have to be given up. No matter which sector (private or public) that produces (or distributes) scarce goods, someone must pay the cost of providing such goods.

As the amount of goods provided by a government increases, so will the total costs of that government. More public goods means more taxes. The link between aggregate consumption and aggregate costs of production cannot be broken by public sector action because of scarcity.

Over the past twenty-five years, there has been a notable trend among African countries for their governments to increase spending. These governments are assuming more and more responsibility for the immediate well-being of their citizens. Public expenditures on education, health, and welfare are rising throughout Africa as citizens come to expect more social concern from their governments. As a result, the planning and finance ministries in Africa, the key agencies involved in project development and policy-making, need reinforcement facilitated by relational models of data if they are to play the important role demanded for economic development.

However, almost in every country in Africa the financial and budgetary instruments of public sectors are overburdened. In addition, there is a high turnover among statisticians in the planning and finance ministries (The World Bank 1981:33). This makes it difficult for the effective execution of government programs and the formulation of coherent policies.

African planning and finance ministries need greater capacity in policy analysis particularly in the areas of tax planning, assessment of budgetary requests, and determination of overall fiscal and monetary policies. The governments should therefore provide these ministries more resources that will enable them to make credible technical contributions to policy decisions at both the sectoral and macroeconomic levels. In addition, incentives should be provided to help stem the rise in turnover among qualified statisticians who are desperately needed to provide much needed data.

The Element of Compulsion in the Public Sector

The dominant characteristic of market organization is voluntary exchange. A minority need not yield to the desires of the majority in the private sector. The views of the majority do not prevent minority consumers from buying desired goods and services.

Unlike large corporations which cannot require a consumer to buy their products, governments have an exclusive right to the use of coercion. When a majority (either directly elected or through the legislative process) decides on a particular policy, the minority (even against its will) must accept the policy and help pay for its costs.

The right to compel is on certain occasions quite necessary to promote social cooperation. For example, legislation compelling drivers not to operate their vehicles while under the influence of alcohol enhances the safety of others. Certain limitations are sometimes necessary to increase social cooperativeness and even expand available options.

The problem in Africa, however, has been one of excessive compulsion. As Chazan and her partners observe, authoritarian politics has dominated the domestic scene in Africa. As they emphasize,

Competition over access to and control of state resources has nurtured an instrumental view of politics in which the public domain is seen as a channel for individual or partisan enrichment. Zero-sum patterns of interaction (one side's gain is another side's loss) have led to the muzzling of loyal oppositions and to an intolerance of dissenting opinions (Chazan et al. 1988:7).

These conditions have made the military an important mechanism of bringing about political change. Virtually every African country has witnessed some form of an attempted coup. And as Bangura (1994) found after a meta-analysis of ninety two studies on Africa's military intervention and military rule, (a) economic condition, domestic environment for political participation, social mobilization, and foreign influence have negative, albeit small, effects on coup d'état outcomes; (b) institutional structure, and pluralism have positive, but small, effects on coup d'état outcomes.

These developments have not improved governments' capacities. The top-heavy administrations run by civilian or military leaders wield very little authority, and the power of their governmental institutions has remained weak. Instability has indeed become the modus operandi throughout post-colonial Africa.

Thus, as argued earlier, democratic governments are needed in Africa to help ensure checks and balances on the public sectors' element of compulsion. An encouraging sign is that the 1980s witnessed the founding of more political parties on the continent. Whether these political parties will help lead to democratic governments remains to be seen.

Collective Legislative Decision-Making

Voters must choose among candidates who represent bundles of positions on issues when collective decisions are made through the legislative process. A voter cannot choose the views of Candidate A on certain issues and simultaneously choose the views of Candidate B who is opposed to the former's positions. Unable to separate a candidate's views on one issue from his views on another, the voter's power to register preferences on specific issues is reduced.

Choosing a representative is a bit like choosing an agent who will both control a substantial portion of one's income and at the same time regulate one's activities. The voter's preferred candidate may or may not be elected. The elected candidate has the responsibility, however, to represent thousands of other persons on each legislative issue.

Education, then, becomes a key factor for enhancing one's ability to analyze each candidate's positions. In short order, an educated voter is a good political consumer. Most countries where education is minimal and literacy is severely limited tend to be undemocratic; they tend to be traditional, adhering to authoritarian and hierarchical values. The illiterate person increasingly finds himself or herself disenfranchised from effective political participation. S/he also becomes barred from the social and economic paths toward a better and more secure life.

In the case of Africa, massive investments in education have paid dividends. Literacy rates have more than doubled in many countries. In Tanzania, rural adult literacy rose from 10 percent to 65 percent between 1961 and 1981. By 1982, primary school enrollments throughout Sub-Saharan Africa averaged 77 percent of the total primary-school age population. Only a small number of countries, Chad, Mali, Burkina Faso, Somalia, Niger, Burundi and Mauritania, had enrollments less than 50 percent of the age group. In a few countries, such as Congo and Gabon, the figures for enrollments were more than 130 percent, reflecting the fact that large numbers of citizens beyond the primary-school age groups were going to school. There was also widespread evidence that traditional prejudice against the education of females was waning as indicated by a weighted mean of 60 percent of the female primary-school age population in 1982 (Chazan et al. 1988:231).

Despite these gains in primary education enrollments, the same cannot be said about secondary and post-secondary education and in other areas like curriculum reform. A number of constraints have hampered African governments in these areas. These include: (a) financial problems, (b) popular expectations of improved access to all levels of schooling, and (c) lack of employment opportunities for secondary-school graduates and for some university graduates (especially those with liberal arts degrees). Some

African governments have been reluctant to increase the output of second-ary-school and university-educated students beyond the short-term per-sonnel needs of their economies in fear of the discontent that would be bred by frustrated expectations (Chazan et al 1988:231).

Reflecting the general educational imbalance in African countries, it may be necessary for the governments to move away from established methods and recast their educational systems to meet their specific needs. Traditional educational approaches which seek to prepare people for rela-tively fixed roles and those that are associated with status must be aban-doned. Different approaches that are geared toward the meeting of modes of skill acquisition and self-determination are to be pursued. Integrating education within their overall development strategies calls for greater emphasis on the wider participation in, and development through, such a changed educational process. This will include both formal and informal processes if education is to be incorporated more directly into the overall development process itself.

Distribution of Income and Power in Both the Market and Public Sectors

Individuals who supply more highly valued resources get larger incomes in the marketplace. The amount of money one receives in this arena reflects his or her abilities, drive, skills, perceptiveness, good fortune, and inheri-tance, among other factors. This results into an unequal distribution of consumer power.

In the public arena, ballots speak when decisions are made democrati-cally. One person, one vote is the name of the game. This does not mean that political goods and services are allocated equally to all citizens by the collective decision-making process. Citizens who are much more astute than others tend to use the political process to obtain personal advantages.

In Africa, social groups have become much more astute over their own particular circumstances. As Chazan and her partners (1988:6) note, ethnic groupings, incipient classes and a number of local communities, professional associations, trade unions, women's organizations, and religious movements have formed to pursue their own interests. In some circumstances, patron-client relationships have emerged to raise demands and to distribute benefits. In other cases, politicization has increased while access to the political center has been severely curtailed. The opportunity for citizen involvement has thus varied greatly from country to country and from time to time.

Since efforts to alter the distribution of income and political power will also affect supply conditions and the political climate, in light of Africa's multi-ethnic states, the issue is highly complex. As long as the preferences and abilities of individuals differ, market or political solutions will lead to unequal distribution of income and power. Thus, incentives should be provided that encourage every citizen to undertake productive activities.

This calls for effective channels of communication to coordinate the actions of citizens and decision-makers, and to provide the incentive structure that motivates decision-makers to act. The information provided will instruct policy-makers as to (a) how to utilize scarce resources and (b) which policies are intensely desired by citizens. A reward-penalty system, which induces individuals to cooperate with each other and motivates them to work efficiently, will help to strengthen the political system. The efficiency of the system will depend on (a) competitive and fair market and political conditions and (b) securely defined private and public property rights.

In sum, the propositions in the foregoing suggestion may be objectionable to those who have insisted that the search for new paths to development in Africa demands that the whole traditional conceptual and theoretical framework of development as derived from the West be replaced by more indigenous development notions. These observers may also argue that Public Choice, being a Western theory, should not be tested in Africa. But herein lies the first problem: How do African governments implement indigenous development policies when the majority of them are dependent on tourism, Western aid, and when even in the villages foreign products are preferred to locally manufactured ones? These are serious concerns for social science in Africa.

A second problem involves the relationship between resource endowments and the sizes of the domestic markets. How, for example, should the great mineral, oil and other natural resource wealth of African countries be utilized? An obvious answer will be export, but this raises the whole issue of dependency.

A third problem is the fact that African political leaders lack the capacity to propose new forms for society or any kind of strategy for coping with the challenge of multinational corporations. In a global economy controlled by a very new form of oligopoly capital which is a more or less all-embracing phenomenon, how can African leaders formulate new strategies to face this serious challenge? Very often proposals by government officials are criticized by some local bourgeoisies who prefer to be directly associated with the multinational corporations.

The suggestion of Public Choice, buttressed by a relational model of data, as a plausible approach to insure accountability for sustained economic development in African nations hinges on the fact that it begins with two fundamental assumptions that are relevant to any society: (1) that all individuals act rationally in their own self-interest, and (2) that all interests are individual economic interests. The two assumptions undoubtedly are objectionable from many points of view. Moreover, given their individualistic, rationalistic and competitive connotations, they appear unlikely to allow for a government based on unanimous consent. But in fact, in conjunction with one another (much more plausible) assumption, they are sufficient to deduce that such a government can exist.

Of course, if other human motives and values are mixed into the initial assumption (the value of political community per se, man is by nature of political animal, etc.) this conclusion can be reached more directly—indeed too directly to be particularly interesting. The point is that this conclusion can be reached even on the basis of these apparently unfruitful assumptions. Essentially, it is necessary to show that common interests exist and, at the same time, that common interests are not always realized in the absence of some form of coercive authority.

Incidentally, African governments perform more than minimal 'night-watchman' functions. These governments collect taxes, spend money, regulate economies, and more. When public goods are present, rational individual actions by participants (the free-rider problem, the bargaining problem, and other bargaining costs) may not produce an optimal outcome. Instead, some measure of explicit cooperation may be required to achieve optimality. When the number of participants is at all large, voluntary cooperative action is difficult to organize and the outcome may remain suboptimal. The existence of governmental authority can help to achieve optimality.

We should note that even laws which win unanimous support (over the status quo) must be enforced, since individuals have incentives to violate them. We should also note that a government based on unanimity rule is not equivalent to no government at all and that such a government can undertake positive activities even in a situation of partially conflicting interests. We can conclude, therefore, that even in a community composed of many politically or economically self-interested groups, establishment of a government with coercive authority can command unanimous consent.

What, then, does Public Choice teach us about development planning? Such an endeavor would take a number of forms. Public Choice's concern for the motives of decision-makers suggests that policies designed to promote development can be expected to be adopted for other reasons such as soliciting support for the government or increasing political control. How will this emerge?

Price and tax policies, for example, designed to encourage investment can be implemented through a relational model of data to enhance the inherent stability of a government. Social overhead capital projects such as roads, irrigation projects, educational programs, etc. can be distributed with a maximum concern for the returns to supporters of a government and to increase the regime's ability to deliver coercion among dissidents. In order to avoid distortions that often lead to wastefulness, sacrifices of some goals are in order. And a series of computer programs can help toward this end. Indeed, a common saying among Public Choice enthusiasts is quite apt: We cannot have our cake and eat it too!

Bibliography

Adelman, I. and C. T. Taft Morris. 1973. *Economic Growth and Social Equity in Developing Countries*. Stanford, California: Stanford University Press.

Aho, A. V., C. Beeri and J, D. Ullman. 1979. The theory of joins in relational databases. *ACM Transactions on Database Systems* 4, 3:297-314.

Aho, A. V., Y. Sagiv and J. D. Ullman. 1979. Efficient optimization of a class of relational expressions. *ACM Transactions on Database Systems* 4, 4:435-454.

Aho, A. V., Y. Sagiv and J. D. Ullman. 1979. Equivalence of relational expressions. *SIAM Journal on Computing* 8, 2:218-246.

Aho, A. V. and J. D. Ullman. 1979. Universality of data retrieval languages. In *Sixth ACM Symposium on Principles of Programming Languages* 110-117.

Alexandrov, V. N. and G. M. Megson. 1999. *Parallel Algorithms for Knapsack Type Problems*. Singapore, Malaysia: World Scientific.

Andrews, G. R. 1991. *Concurrent Programming: Principles and Practice*. Menlo Park, California: Addison-Wesley Publishing Company.

Apt, K. R. 1997. *From Logic Programming to Prolog*. London, England: Prentice Hall.

Apt, K. R. and F. Turini. 1995. *Meta-Logics and Logic Programming*. Cambridge, Massachusetts: The MIT Press.

Apt, K. R. et al., eds. 1999. *The Logic Programming: A 25-Year Perspective*. Berlin, Germany: Springer.

Armstrong, W. W. 1974. Dependency structure of database relationships. *IFIP Congress* 580-583.

Armstrong, W. W. and C. Delobel. 1980. Decompositions and functional dependencies in relations. *ASCM Transactions on Database Systems* 5, 4:404-430.

Arrow, K. J. 1951. *Social Choice and Individual Values*. New York, New York: Wiley.

Asperti, A. and S. Guerrini. 1998. *The Optimal Implementation of Functional Programming Languages*. Cambridge, Great Britain: Cambridge University Press.

Atzeni, P. and V. De Antonellis. 1993. *Relational Database Theory*. Redwood City, CA: The Benjamin/Cummings Publishing Company, Inc.

Atzeni, P., et al. 1982. Inclusion and equivalence between relational database schemata. *Theoretical Computer Science* 19, 2::267-285.

Atzeni, P. and E. P. F. Chan. 1989. Efficient optimization of simple chase join expressions. *ACM Transactions on Database Systems* 14, 2:212-230.

Atzeni, P. and E. P. F. Chan. 1985. Efficient query answering in the representative instance approach. *Fourth ACM SIGACT SIGMOD Symposium on Principles of Database Systems*. 181-188.

Atzeni, P. and M. C. De Bernadis. 1990. A new interpretation for null values in the weak instance model. *Journal of Computer and Systems Science* 41, 1:25-43.

Atzeni, P. and M. C. De Bernadis. 1987. A new basis for the weak instance model. *Sixth ACM SIGACT SIGMOD SIGART Symposium on Principles of Database Systems* 79-86.

Atzeni, P. and N. M. Morfuni. 1986. Functional dependencies and constraints on null values in database relations. *Information and Control* 70, 1:1-31.

Atzeni, P. and N. M. Morfuni. 1984. Functional dependencies in relations with null values. *Information Processing Letters* 18, 4:233-238.

Atzeni, P. and D. S. Parker, Jr. 1982. Assumptions in relational database theory. *ACM SIGACT SIGMOD Symposium on Principles of Database Systems* 1-9.

Atzeni, P. and R. Torlone. 1990. Efficient updates to independent database schemes in the weak instance model. *ACM SIGMOD International Conference on Management of Data* 84-93.

Atzeni, P. and R. Torlone. 1989. Updating databases in the weak instance model. *Eighth ACM SIGACT SIGMOD SIGART Symposium on Principles of Database Systems* 101-109.

Axford, T. 1989. *Concurrent Programming: Fundamental Techniques for Real-Time and Parallel Software Design*. Chichester, England: John Wiley and Sons.

Babb, R. G. II, ed. 1988. *Programming Parallel Processors*. Reading, Massachusetts: Addison-Wesley Publishing Company, Inc.

Babbie, E. 1998. *The Practice of Social Research*, 6th ed. Belmont, CA: Wadsworth Publishing Company.

Banâtre, J.-P. et al. 1991. *Prospects for Functional Programming in Software Engineering*. Berlin, Germany: Springer-Verlag.

Bancilhon, F. 1978. On the completeness of query languages for relational databases. *Mathematical Foundations of Computer Science, LNCS 64*. Berlin: Springer-Verlag 112-124.

Bangura, A. K. 1995. *The Effects of American Foreign Aid to Egypt, 1957-1987*. Lewinston, New York: The Edwin Mellen Press.

Bangura, A. K. 1994. Explaining and predicting the causes of military coups d'état in Africa: A meta-analysis. In A. K. Bangura, ed. *Research Methodology and African Studies*. Lanham, Maryland: University Press of America.

Bauer, B. E. 1992. *Practice Parallel Programming*. San Diego, California: Academic Press, Inc.

Beeri, C. 1988. Data models and languages for databases. *ICDT '88, Second International Conference on Data Base Theory, Bruges, Lecture Notes in Computer Science 326*. Berlin: Springer-Verlag 19037.

Beeri, C. and P. A. Bernstein. 1979. Computational problems related to the design of normal form relational schemes. *ACM Transactions on Database Systems*. 4, 1:30-59.

Beeri, C., P. A. Bernstein and N. Goodman. 1978. A sophisticate's introduction to database normalization theory. *Fourth International Conference on Very Large Data Bases,* Berlin 113-124.

Beeri, C., R. Fagin and J. H. Howard. 1978. A complete axiomatization for functional and multivalued dependencies. *ACM SIGMOD International Conference on Management of Data* 47-61.

Beeri, C. and P. Honeyman. 1981. Preserving functional dependencies. *SIAM Journal on Computing* 10, 3:647-656.

Beeri, C. and M. Kifer. 1986. An integrated approach to logical design of relational database schemes. *ACM Transactions on Database Systems* 1, 2:134-158.

Beeri, C. et al. 1981. Equivalence of relational database schemes. *SIAM Journal on Computing* 10, 2:352-370.

Beeri, C. and J. Rissanen. 1980. Faithful representation of relational database schemata. Report RJ 2722. IBM Research, San Jose.

Beeri, C. and M. Y. Vardi. 1984. Formal systems for tuple and equality-generating dependencies. *SIAM Journal on Computing* 13, 1:76-98.

Beeri, C. and M. Y. Vardi. 1984. A proof procedure for data dependencies. *Journal of the ACM* 31, 4:718-741.

Bergadano, F. and D. Gunetti. 1996. *Inductive Logic Programming.* Cambridge, Massachusetts: The MIT Press.

Bernstein, A. J. and P. M. Lewis. 1993. *Concurrency in Programming and Database Systems.* Boston, Massachusetts: Jones and Bartlett Publishers.

Bernstein, P. A. 1976. Synthesizing third normal form relations from functional dependencies. *ACM Transactions on Database Systems* 1, 4:277-298.

Bernstein, P. A. and N. Goodman. 1980. What does Boyce-Codd normal form do? *Sixth International Conference on Very Large Data Bases,* Montreal 245-259.

Biskup, J. 1983. A foundation of Codd's relational maybe-operations. *ACM Transactions on Database Systems* 8, 4:608-636.

Biskup, J. 1981. A formal approach to null values in database relations. G. Gallaire et al. eds. *Advances in Database Theory*, New York: Plenum, 299-341.

Biskup, J., U. Dayal and P. A. Bernstein. 1979. Synthesizing independent database schemes. *ACM SIGMOD International Conference on Management of Data* 143-151.

Black, D. 1958. *The Theory of Committees and Elections*. Cambridge, England: Cambridge University Press.

Black, D. 1951. *Committee Decisions with Complementary Valuation*. London, England: W. Hodge.

Blair, G. et al., eds. 1991. *Object-Oriented Languages, Systems and Applications*. New York, New York: Halsted Press, an imprint of John Wiley and Sons, Inc.

Booch, G. 1994. *Object-Oriented Analysis and Design with Applications*, 2nd ed. Reading, Massachusetts: Addison-Wesley Publishing Company.

Brathwaite, K. S. 1991. *Relational Databases: Concepts, Design, and Administration*. New York: McGraw-Hill, Inc.

Braud, E. J., ed. 1998. *Object Oriented Analysis, Design and Testing*. Piscataway, New Jersey: IEEE, Inc.

Brawer, S. 1989. *Introduction to Parallel Programming*. Boston, Massachusetts: Academic Press, Inc.

Buchanan, J. M. 1969. *The Demand and Supply of Public Goods*. Chicago, Illinois: Rand McNally.

Buchanan, J. M. 1967. *Public Finance in Democratic Process*. Chapel Hill, North Carolina: University of North Carolina Press.

Buchanan, J. M. and R. D. Tollison, eds. 1972. *Theory of Public Choice*. Ann Arbor, Michigan: University of Michigan Press.

Buchanan, J. M. and G. Tullock. 1967. *Calculus of Consent*. Ann Arbor, Michigan: University of Michigan Press.

Bullock, C. S. III. 1972. House careerists: Changing patterns of longevity and attrition. *American Political Science Review* 66.

Burn, G. 1991. *Lazy Functional Languages: Abstract Interpretation and Compilation*. Cambridge, Massachusetts: The MIT Press.

Burnett, M., A. Goldberg and T. G. Lewis. 1995. *Visual Object-Oriented Programming*. Greenwich, Connecticut: Manning Publications Company.

Burns, A. 1988. *Programming in Occam 2*. Wokingham, England: Addison-Wesley Publishing Company.

Cacace, F. and G. Lamperti. 1996. *Advanced Relational Programming*. Dordrecht, The Netherlands: Kluwer Academic Publishers.

Caneghem, M. V. and D. H. D. Warren, eds. 1986. *Logic Programming and Its Applications*. Norwood, New Jersey: Ablex Publishing Corporation.

Carriero, N. and D. Gelernter. 1990. *How to Write Parallel Program: A First Course*. Cambridge, Massachusetts: The MIT Press.

Casanova, M. A. 1981. The theory of functional and subset dependencies over relational expressions. Technical Report 3/81. Rio de Janeiro: Dep. De Informatica, Pontifica Universidade Catolica.

Casanova, M. A., R. Fagin and C. H. Papadimitriou. 1984. Inclusion dependencies and their interaction with functional dependencies. *Journal of Computer and Systems Science* 28, 1:29-59.

Ceri, S., G. Gottlob and L. Tanca. 1990. *Logic Programming and Databases*. Berlin, Germany: Springer-Verlag.

Chamberlain, D. D. et al. 1981. A history and evaluation of System R. *Communications of the ACM* 24, 10.

Chan, E. P. F. 1989. A design theory for solving the anomalies problem. *SIAM Journal on Computing* 18, 3:429-448.

Chan, E. P. F.1984. Optimal computation of total projections with unions of simple chase join expressions. *ACM SIGMOD International Conference on Management of Data* 149-163.

Chan, E. P. F. and H. Hernández. 1988. On the desirability of -acyclic BCNF database schemes. *Theoretical Computer Science* 62, 1-2.

Chan, E. P. F. and A. O. Mendelzon. 1987. Independent and separable database schemes. *SIAM Journal on Computing* 16, 5:841-851.

Chanda, K. M. and J. Misra. 1988. *Parallel Program Design: A Foundation.* Reading, Massachusetts: Addison-Wesley Publishing Company,

Chandra, A. K. 1988. Theory of database queries. *Seventh ACM SIGACT SIGMOD SIGART Symposium on Principles of Database Systems* 1-9.

Chandra, A. K. and D. Harel. 1980. Computable queries for relational databases. *Journal of Computer and System Sciences* 21:333-347.

Chandra, A. K., H. R. Lewis and J. A. Makowsky. 1981. Embedded implicational dependencies and their inference problem. *Thirteenth ACM SIGACT Symposium on Theory of Computing* 342-354.

Chandra, A. K. and M. Y. Vardi. 1985. The implication problem for functional and inclusion dependencies is undecidable. *SIAM Journal on Computing* 14, 3:671-677.

Chazan, N. et al. 1988. *Politics and Society in Contemporary Africa.* Boulder, Colorado: Lynne Riener Publishers.

Chenery, H. B. and M. Bruno. 1962. Development alternatives in an open economy: The case of Israel. *Economic Journal* March, 79-103.

Chenery, H. B. and I. Adelman. 1966a. Foreign aid and economic development: The case of Greece. *Review of Economics and Statistics* xlviii, 1:1-19.

Chenery, H. B. and I. Adelman. 1966b. Trade, aid and economic development. In S. H. Robock and L. M. Solomon, eds. *International Development.* Bobbs Ferry, New York: Oceana Publications.

Chenery, H. B. and A. M. Strout. 1966c. Foreign assistance and economic development. *American Economic Review* lvi, 4:679-733.

Chenery, H. B. and P. Ekstein. 1970. Development alternatives for Latin America. *Journal of Political Economy* July/August, 966-1006.

Chenery, H. B. et al. 1974. *Redistribution with Growth.* New York, New York: Oxford University Press.

Clark, K. L. and S.-A. Tärlund, eds. 1982. *Logic Programming*. London, England: Academic Press, Inc.

Codd, E. F. 1988. 'Universal' relation fails to replace relational model. Letter to the editor. *IEEE Software* 5, 4:4-6.

Codd, E. F. 1979. Extending the database relational model to capture more meaning. *ACM Transactions on Database Systems* 4, 4:397-434.

Codd, E. F. 1974. Recent investigations into relational database systems. *IFIP Congress* 1017-1021.

Codd, E. F. 1972. Relational completeness of data base sublanguages. R. Rustin, ed. *Data Base Systems*. Englewood Cliffs, NJ: Prentice-Hall, Inc., 65-98.

Codd, E. F. 1972. Further normalization of the data base relational model. R. Rustin, ed. *Data Base Systems*. Englewood Cliffs, NJ: Prentice-Hall, Inc.

Codd, E. F. 1971. A database sublanguage founded on the relational calculus. *ACM SIGFIDET Workshop on Data Description, Access and Control* 35-61.

Codd, E. F. 1970. A relational model for large shared data banks. *Communications of the ACM* 13, 6:377-387.

Cok, R. S. 1991. *Parallel Programs for the Transputer*. Englewood Cliffs, New Jersey: Prentice-Hall, Inc.

Coleman, J. S. 1966. Individual interests and collective action. In G. Tullock, ed. *Papers on Non-Market Decision-Making*. Charlottesville, Virginia: Thomas Jefferson Center for Political Economy, University of Virginia.

Conery, J. S. 1987. *Parallel Execution of Logic Programs*. Boston, Massachusetts: Kluwer Academic Publishers.

Couseneau, G. and M. Mauny. 1998. *The Functional Approach to Programming*. Cambridge, Great Britain: Cambridge University Press.

Dahmke, M. 1986. *Using Concurrent PC DOS*. New York, New York: McGraw-Hill Book Company.

Date, C. J. 1987. *A Guide to INGRESS*. Reading, MA: Addison Wesley.

Date, C. J. 1986. *An Introduction to Database Systems*, 4th ed., vol. 1. Reading, MA: Addison Wesley.

Date, C. J. 1984. *A Guide to DB2*. Reading, MA: Addison Wesley.

Date, C. J. 1983. *An Introduction to Database Systems*, vol. 2. Reading, MA: Addison Wesley.

Date, C. J. with H. Darwen. 1992. *Relational Database Writings 1989-1991*. Reading, Massachusetts: Addison-Wesley Publishing Company.

DeBra, P. and J. Paredaens. 1984. Horizontal decompositions for handling exceptions to functional dependencies. H. Gallaire, J. Minker and J.-M. Nicolas, eds. *Advances in Database Theory*, vol. 2. New York: Plenum Books, 123-144.

DeBra, P. and J. Paredaens. 1983. An algorithm for horizontal decompositions. *Information Processing Letters* 17, 2:91-95.

Deepak, L. 1974. *Methods of Project Analysis: A Review*. Baltimore, Maryland: Johns Hopkins University Press.

Delobel, C. and R. C. Casey. 1972. Decomposition of a database and the theory of Boolean switching functions. *IBM Journal of Research and Development* 17, 5:370-386.

Doets, K. 1994. *From Logic to Logic Programming*. Cambridge, Massachusetts: The MIT Press.

Downs, A. 1960. Why the government budget is too small in a democracy. *World Politics* 12, 4.

Downs, A. 1957. *An Economic Theory of Democracy*. New York, New York: Harper and Row.

ElMasri, R. A. and S. B. Navathe. 1988. *Fundamentals of Database Systems*. Menlo Park, CA: Benjamin/Cummings.

Fagin, R. 1982. Horn clauses and database dependencies. *Journal of the ACM* 29, 4:952-983.

Fagin, R. 1981. A normal form for relational databases that is based on domains and keys. *ACM Transactions on Database Systems* 6, 3:310-319.

Fagin, R. 1979. Normal forms and relational databases operators. *ACM SIGMOD International Conference on Management of Data* 123-134.

Fagin, R. 1977. Multivalued dependencies and a new normal form for relational databases. *ACM Transactions on Database Systems* 2, 3:262-278.

Fagin, R. 1977. The decomposition versus the synthetic approach to relational database design. *Third International Conference on Very Large Data Bases, Tokyo* 441-446.

Fagin, R, A. O. Mendelzon and J. D. Ullman. 1982. A simplified universal relation assumption and its properties. *ACM Transactions on Database Systems* 7, 3:343-360.

Fayad, M. and M. Laitinen. 1998. *Transition to Object-Oriented Software Development*. New York, New York: John Wiley and Sons, Inc.

Gabbay, D. M., C. J. Hogger and J. A. Robinson. 1995. *Handbook of Logic in Artificial Intelligence and Logic Programming*, vol. 4. Oxford, England: Clarendon Press.

Gardarin, G. and P. Valduriez. 1989. *Relational Databases and Knowledge Bases*. Reading, Massachusetts: Addison-Wesley Publishing Company.

Gehani, N. and A. D. McGettrick, eds. 1988. *Concurrent Programming*. Wokingham, England: Addison-Wesley Publishing Company.

Goldberg, A. 1984. *Smalltalk-80: The Interactive Programming Environment*. Reading, Massachusetts: Addison-Wesley Publishing Company.

Goldstein, B. S. 1981. Constraints on null values in relational databases. *Seventh International Conference on Very Large Data Bases* 101-111.

Graham, M., A. O. Mendelzon, and M. Y. Vardi. 1986. Notions of dependency satisfaction. *Journal of ACM* 33, 1:105-129.

Graham, M. and M. Yannakakis. 1984. Independent database schema. *Journal of Comp. and System Sc.* 28, 1:121-141.

Grant, J. 1977. Null values in a relational database. *Information Processing Letters* 6, 5:156-159.

Grill, E. 1990. *Relational Databases: A Methodical Guide for Practical Design and Implementation*. New York: Ellis Horwood.

Gwartney, J. D. and R. Stroup. 1983. *Microeconomics: Private and Public Choice*, 3rd ed. New York, New York: Academic Press.

Halladay, S. and M. Wiebel. 1993. *Object-Oriented Software Engineering*. Lawrence, Kansas: R & D Publications, Inc.

Hansen, J. L. 1978. *Guide to Practical Project Appraisal: Social Benefit-Cost Analysis in Developing Countries*. New York, New York: United Nations Publications.

Hansen, P. B. 1977. *The Architecture of Concurrent Programs*. Englewood Cliffs, New Jersey: Prentice-Hall, Inc.

Hares, J. S. and J. D. Smart. 1994. *Object Orientation: Technology, Techniques, Management and Migration*. New York, New York: John Wiley and Sons.

Harrison, M. A. 1978. *Introduction to Formal Language Theory*. Reading, Massachusetts: Addison-Wesley Publishing Company.

Hartman, A. C. 1977. *A Concurrent Pascal Compiler for Microcomputers*. Berlin, Germany: Springer-Verlag.

Hernández, H. and E. P. F. Chan. 1991. Constant-time-maintainable BCNF database schemes. *ACM Trans. on Database Syst.* 16, 4:571-599.

Hettne, B. 1978. *Current Issues in Development Theory*. Gothenburg, Sweden: SAREC.

Hettne, B. and P. Wallensteen. 1978. *Emerging Trends in Development Theory*. Gothenburg, Sweden: SAREC.

Hoare, C. A. R. and J. C. Shepherdson, eds. 1985. *Mathematical Logic Programming Languages*. Englewood Cliffs, New Jersey: Prentice/Hall International

Hogger, C. J. 1990. *Essentials of Logic Programming*. Oxford, England: Clarendon Press.

Honeyman, P. 1982. Testing satisfaction of functional dependencies. *Journal of the ACM* 29, 3:666-677.

Howie, J. M. 1991. *Automata and Languages*. Oxford, England: Clarendon Press.

Hull, R. 1988. A survey of theoretical research on typed complex database objects. In J. Paredaens, ed. *Databases*. New York, New York: Academic Press.

Hull, R. B. 1986. Relative information capacity of simple relational schemata. *SIAM Journal on Computing* 15, 3:856-886.

Hunt, J. 1997. *Smalltalk and Object Orientation: An Introduction*. Berlin, Germany: Springer-Verlag.

Imielinski, T. and W. Lipski. 1981. On representing incomplete information in relational databases. *Seventh International Conf. on Very Large Data Bases* 388-397.

Imielinski, T. and W. Lipski. 1983. Incomplete information and dependencies in relational databases. *ACM SIGMOD International Conference on Management of Data* 178-184.

Irvin, G. 1978. *Modern Cost-Benefit Methods*. Thousand Oaks, California: Sage Publications.

Ito, M., M. Iwasaki and T. Kasami. 1985. Some results on the representative instance in relational databases. *SIAM Journal on Computing* 14, 2:334-354.

Jamieson, L. H., D. B. Gannon and R. J. Douglass, eds. 1987. *The Characteristics of Parallel Algorithms*. Cambridge, Massachusetts: The MIT Press.

Jou, J. H. and P. C. Fischer. 1983. The complexity of recognizing 3NF relation schemes. *Information Processing Letters* 14, 4:187-190.

Joyner, I. 1999. *Objects Unescapsulated: JAVA, EIFFEL, and C++??*. Upper Saddle River, New Jersey: Prentice Hall PTR.

Justo, G. R. R. 1996. *Introduction to Parallel Programming Languages and Occam*. (Http://www.cpc.wmin.ac.uk/ParallelCourse/ Course/ Course.html).

Kaehler, T. and D. Patterson. 1986. *A Taste of Smalltalk*. New York, New York: W. W. Norton and Company.

Kandzia, P. and H. Klein. 1979. On equivalence of relational databases in connection with normalization. *Workshop on Formal Bases for Databases*. Toulouse: ONERA-CERT.

Kanellakis, P. C., S. Cosmadakis and M. Vardi. 1983. Unary inclusion dependencies have polynomial-time inference problems. *Fifteenth ACM SIGACT Symp. on Theory of Computing* 164-277.

Kaplan, A. 1964. *The Conduct of Inquiry*. San Francisco, CA: Chandler Publishing Company.

Kaufmann, W. J. and L. L. Smarr. 1993. *Supercomputing and the Transformation of Science*. New York, New York: Scientific American Library, a division of W. H. Freeman and Company.

Keller, A. M. 1986. Set-theoretic problems of null completion in relational databases. *Information Processing Letters* 22, 5:261-265.

Kelly, P. 1989. *Functional Programming for Loosely-coupled Multiprocessors*. Cambridge, Massachusetts: The MIT Press.

Kent, W. 1981. Consequences of assuming a universal relation. *ACM Trans. on Database Syst.* 6, 4:539-556.

Kent, W. 1983. The universal relation revisited. *ACM Trans. on Database Syst.* 8, 4:644-648.

Klug, A. 1982. Equivalence of relational algebra and relational calculus query languages having aggregate functions. *Journal of the ACM* 29, 3:699-717.

Koopman, P. J., Jr. 1990. *An Architecture for Combinator Graph Reduction*. Boston, Massachusetts: Academic Press, Inc.

Korth, H. F. and A. Silberschatz. 1986. *Database Systems Concepts*. New York, New York: McGraw-Hill.

Korth, H. F. and J. D. Ullman. 1980. System U: A system based on the universal relation assumption. XP1 Workshop on Relational Database Theory, State University of New York, Stonybrook, New York.

Kung, D., P. Hsia and J. Gao. 1998. *Testing Object-Oriented Software*. Los Alamitos, California: IEEE Computer Society Press.

Lacroix, M. and A. Pirotte. 1976. Generalized joins. *ACM SIGMOD Record* 8, 3:14-15.

Lakshmivarahan, S. and S. K. Dhall. 1990. *Analysis and Design of Parallel Algorithms: Arithmetic and Matrix Problems*. New York, New York: McGraw-Hill Publishing Company.

Lavra, N. and S. Deroski. 1994. *Inductive Logic Programming*. New York, New York: Ellis Horwood.

LeDoux, C. H. and D. S. Parker. 1982. Reflections on Boyce-Codd normal form. *Eighth International Conf. on Very Large Data Bases* 131-141.

Legum, C. et al. 1979. *Africa in the 1980s* New York, New York: McGraw-Hill Book Company.

Lerat, N. and W. Lipski, Jr. 1986. Nonapplicable nulls. *Theoretical Computer Science* 46, 1:67-82.

Levi, G., ed. 1994. *Advances in Logic Programming*. Oxford, England: Clarendon Press.

Lieberherr, K. J. 1996. *Adaptive Object-Oriented Software: The Demeter Method with Propagation Patterns*. Boston, Massachusetts: PWS Publishing Company, on International Thomson Publishing Company.

Lieberman, E. R. 1991. *Multi-Objective Programming in the USSR*. Boston, Massachusetts: Academic Press.

Lien, Y. E. 1982. On the equivalence of database models. *Journal of the ACM* 29, 2:333-362.

Lien, Y. E. 1979. Multivalued dependencies with null values in relational databases. *Fifth International Conf. on Very Large Data Bases* 61-66.

Lipski, W. Jr. 1981. On databases with incomplete information. *Journal of the ACM* 28, 1:41-70.

Lipski, W. Jr. 1979. On semantic issues connected with incomplete information databases. *ACM Trans. on Database Syst.* 4, 3:262- 296.

Lipski, W. Jr. 1977. Two NP-complete problems related to information retrieval. *Fundamentals of Computation Theory, Lecture Notes in Computer Science* 56. Berlin, Germany: Springer-Verlag, 452-458.

Little, I. M. D. and J. A. Mirrlees. 1974. *Project Appraisal and Planning for Developing Countries.* London, England: Heineman.

Little, I. M. D. and D. G. Tipping. 1972. *A Social Cost Benefit Analysis of the Kulai Oil Palm Estate.* Washington, DC: OECD Development Center Publication.

Lloyd, J. W. 1987. *Foundations of Logic Programming,* 2nd extended ed. Berlin, Germany: Springer-Verlag.

Lobo, J., J. Minker and A. Rakasekar. 1992. *Foundations of Disjunctive Logic Programming.* Cambridge, Massachusetts: The MIT Press.

MacLennan, B. J. 1990. *Functional Programming: Practice and Theory.* Reading, Massachusetts: Addison-Wesley Publishing Company.

Magee, J. and J. Kramer. 1999. *Concurrence: State Models and Java Programs.* Chichester, England: John Wiley and Sons.

Maier, D. 1983. *The Theory of Relational Databases.* Potomac, Maryland: Computer Science Press.

Maier, D. 1980. Discarding the universal relation assumption: Preliminary report. XP1 Workshop on Relational Database Theory, State University of New York, Stonybrook, New York.

Maier, D. 1980. Minimum covers in the relational database model. *Journal of the ACM* 27, 4:664-674.

Maier, D., A. O. Mendelzon, F. Sadri and J. D. Ullman. 1980. Adequacy of decompositions in relational databases. *Journal of Computer and Syst. Sc.* 21, 3:368-379.

Maier, D., A. O. Mendelzon and Y. Sagiv. 1979. Testing implications of data dependencies. *ACM Trans. on Database Syst.* 4, 4:455-468.

Maier, D., D. Rozenshtein and D. S. Warren. 1986. Window functions. In P. C. Kanellakis and F. P. Preparata, eds. *Advances in Computing Research* vol. 3. Greenwich, Connecticut: JAI Press 213-246.

Maier, D. and J. D. Ullman. 1981. Fragments of relations: First hack. XP2 Workshop on Relational Database Theory, Penn State University, State College, Pennsylvania.

Maier, D., J. D. Ullman and M. Vardi. 1984. On the foundations of the universal relation model. *ACM Trans. on Database Syst.* 9, 2:283-308.

Manna, Z. 1980. *Lectures on the Logic of Computer Programming.* Philadelphia, Pennsylvania: Society for Industrial and Applied Mathematics.

Manna, Z. and R. Waldinger. 1985. *The Logical Basis for Programming,* vol. 1. Reading, Massachusetts: Addison-Wesley Publishing Company.

Manna, Z. et al. 1977. *Studies in Automatic Programming Logic.* New York, New York: Elsevier North-Holland, Inc.

Mayhew, D. R. 1974. *Congress: The Electoral Connection*, New Haven, Connecticut: Yale University Press.

McKeown, P. G. 1988. *Living with Computers*, 2nd ed. San Diego, California: Harcourt Brace Jovanovich Publishers.

Mendelson, E. 1978. *Introduction to Mathematical Logic.* New York, New York: Van Nostrand-Reinhold.

Mendelzon, A. O. 1984. Database states and their tableaux. *ACM Trans. on Database Syst.* 9. 2:264-282.

Milutonovi, Velijko M., ed. 1988. *Computer Architecture.* New York, New York: Science Publishing Company.

Mishan, E. J. 1976. *Elements of Cost-Benefit Analysis.* New York, New York: Praeger Publishers.

Mitchell, J. C. 1983. The implication problem for functional and inclusion dependencies. *Information and Control* 56, 1:154-173.

Moret, B. M. 1998. *The Theory of Computation.* Reading, Massachusetts: Addison-Wesley Longman, Inc.

Morna, C. L. 1990. Africa's campuses lead pro-democracy drives? *The Chronicle of Higher Education* xxxvii, 13:A1, A40.

Morris, S. 1994. *Object Oriented Programming Under Windows.* Boston, Massachusetts: Butterworth Heinemann.

Nash, H. T. 1958. *American Foreign Policy*, 3rd ed. Homewood, Illinois: Dorsey Press.

Nisbet, R. A. 1969. *Social Change and History*. New York, New York: Oxford University Press.

Niskanen, W. A. 1971. *Bureaucracy and Representative Government*. New York, New York: Aldine-Atherton.

Olson, M. 1965 & 1967. *The Logic of Collective* Action. Cambridge, Massachusetts: Harvard University Press.

Osterhaug, A., ed. 1989. *Guide to Parallel Programming in Sequent Computer Systems*, 2nd ed. Englewood Cliffs, New Jersey: Prentice- Hall, Inc.

Palsberg, J. and M. I. Schwartzbach. 1994. *Object-Oriented Type Systems*. New York, New York: John Wiley and Sons.

Paredaens, J. 1977. About functional dependencies in a database structure and their coverings. Report 342. Philips MBLE Lab.

Paredaens, J. 1978. On the expressive power of the relational algebra. *Information Processing Letters* 7, 2:107-111.

Paulson, L. C. 1991. *ML for the Working Programmer*. Cambridge, Great Britain: Cambridge University Press.

Peyton Jones, S. L. et al., eds. 1990. *Functional Programming, Glasgow 1990*. London, England: Springer-Verlag.

Pirotte, A. 1978. High-level database languages. In H. Gallaire and J. Minker, eds. *Logic and Databases*. New York: Plenum 409-435.

Plasmeijer, R. and M. Van Eekelen. 1993. *Functional Programming and Parallel Graph Rewriting*. Wokingham, England: Addison- Wesley Publishing Company.

Prest, A. R. and R. Turvey. 1975. Cost benefit analysis: A survey. *Economic Journal* (December).

Ragsdale, S., ed. 1991. *Parallel Programming*. New York, New York: McGraw-Hill, Inc.

Reade, C. 1989. *Elements of Functional Programming*. Wokingham, England: Addison-Wesley Publishing Company.

Reilly, M. H. 1990. *A Performance Monitor for Parallel Programs*. Boston, Massachusetts: Academic Press, Inc.

Reppy, J. H. 1999. *Concurrent Programming in ML*. Cambridge, United Kingdom: Cambridge University Press.

Rissanen, J. 1982. Independent components of relations. *ACM Trans. on database Syst.* 2, 4:317-325.

Rissanen, J. 1982. On equivalence of database schemes. *ACM SIGACT SIGMOD Symp. on Principles of Database Systems* 23-26.

Rissanen, J. 1979. Theory of joins for relational databases—a tutorial survey. *Mathematical Foundations of Computer Science, Lecture Notes in Computer Science* 46. Berlin, Germany: Springer-Verlag 537- 551.

Rissanen, J. and C. Delobel. 1973. Decomposition of files, a basis for data storage and retrieval. Report RJ 1220. IBM Research, San Jose, California.

Rosenberg, J. and D. Koch, eds. 1990. *Persistent Object Systems*. New York, New York: Springer-Verlag.

Rostow, W. W. 1960. *The Stages of Economic Growth: A Non-Communist Manifesto*. Cambridge, England: Cambridge University Press.

Russell, C. S. ans N. K. Nicholson, eds. 1981. *Public Choice and Rural Development*. Washington, DC: Resources for the Future.

Sadri, F. and J. D. Ullman. 1982. Template dependencies: A large class of dependencies in the relational model and its complete axiomatization. *Journal of the ACM* 29, 2:363-372.

Sagiv, Y. 1991. Evaluation of queries in independent database schemes. *Journal of the ACM* 38, 1:120-161.

Sagiv, Y. 1983. A characterization of globally consistent databases and their correct access paths. *ACM Trans. on Database Systems* 8, 2:266-286.

Sagiv, Y. 1981. Can we use the universal instance assumption without using nulls? *ACM SIGMOD International Conf. on Management of Data* 108-120.

Saint-Dizier, P. 1994. *Advanced Logic Programming for Language Processing*. London, England: Academic Press Limited.

Saint-Dizier P. and S. Szpakowicz, eds. 1990. *Logic and Logic Grammars for Language Processing*. New York, New York: Ellis Horwood.

Schneider, F. B. 1997. *On Concurrent Programming*. New York, New York: Springer.

Schumpeter, J. A. 1950. *Capitalism, Socialism, and Democracy*, 3rd ed. New York, New York: Harper Torchbooks.

Sciore, E. 1982. A complete axiomatization of full join dependencies. *Journal of the ACM* 29, 2:373-393.

Sciore, E. 1980. The universal instance and database design (Ph.D. Dissertation, Princeton University). Princeton, New Jersey.

Silberschatz, A., M. Stonebraker and J. D. Ullman. 1991. Database systems: Achievements and opportunities. *Communications of the ACM* 34, 10:110-120.

Simovici, D. A. and R. L. Tenney. 1995. *Relational Database Systems*. San Diego, California: Academic Press.

Sinnott, J. D. et al. 1983. *Applied Research in Aging: A Guide to Methods and Resources*. Boston, MA: Little, Brown and Company.

Smith, D. M. 1995. *IBM Smalltalk: The Language*. Redwood City, California: The Benjamin/Cummings Publishing Company, Inc.

Smith, J. M. and D. C. P. Smith. 1977. Database abstractions: Aggregation and generalization. *ACM Trans. on Database Syst.* 2, 2:105-133.

Stonebraker, M. 1989. Future trends in database systems. *IEEE Trans. on Knowledge and Data Eng.* 1, 1:33-44.

Stonebraker, M., ed. 1986. *The INGRES Papers*. Reading, Massachusetts: Addison-Wesley.

Stonebraker, M. and G. Kemnitz. 1991. The Postgress next-generation database management system. *Communications of the ACM* 34, 10:78- 93.

Szmanski, B. K., ed. 1991. *Parallel Functional Languages and Compilers*. New York, New York: ACM Press.

The World Bank. 1981. *Accelerated Development in Sub-Saharan Africa*. Washington, DC: The World Bank.

Tkach, D. and R. Puttick. 1996. *Object Technology in Application Development*, 2nd ed. Redwood City, California: The Benjamin/Cummings Publishing Company, Inc.

Traub, K. R. 1991. *Implementation of Non-Strict Functional Programming Languages*. Cambridge, Massachusetts: The MIT Press.

Treleanen, P. C., ed. 1990. *Parallel Computers: Object-Oriented, Functional, Logic*. Chichester, England: John Wiley and Sons.

Tullock, G. 1966. *Toward a Mathematics of Politics*. Ann Arbor, Michigan: University of Michigan Press.

Tullock, G. 1965. *The Politics of Bureaucracy*. Washington, DC: Public Affairs Press.

Ullman, J. D. 1989. *Principles of Database and Knowledge Base Systems* vol. 2. Potomac, Maryland: Computer Science Press.

Ullman, J. D. 1988. *Principles of Database and Knowledge Base Systems* vol. 1. Potomac, Maryland: Computer Science Press.

Ullman, J. D. 1985. Implementation of logical query languages for databases. *ACM Trans. on Database Syst.* 10, 3:289-321.

Ullman, J. D. 1983. On Kent's 'Consequences of assuming a universal relation.' *ACM Trans. on Database Syst.* 8, 4:637-643.

Ullman, J. D. 1982. Principles *of Database Systems*. Potomac, Maryland: Computer Science Press.

Ullman, J. D. 1982. *Principles of database Systems* vol . 2. Potomac, Maryland: Computer Science Press.

Ullman, J. D. 1982. The U. R. strikes back. *ACM SIGACT SIGMOD Symp. on Principles of Database Systems* 10-22.

UNIDO. 1972. *Guidelines for Project Evaluation*. New York, New York: United Nations Publications.

Valduriez, P. and G. Gardarin. 1989. *Analysis and Comparison of Relational Database Systems*. Reading, Massachusetts: Addison- Wesley.

Vardi, M. Y. 1988. Response to a letter to the editor. *IEEE Software* 5, 4:4-6.

Vardi, M. Y. 1988. The universal relation data model for logical independence. *IEEE Software* 5, 2:80-85.

Vardi, M. Y. 1984. The implication and finite implication problems for typed template dependencies. *Journal of Comp. and System Sc.* 28, 1:3-28.

Vardi, M. Y. 1981. The decision problem for database dependencies. *Information Processing Letters* 12, 5:251-254.

Vassiliou, Y. 1980. A formal treatment of imperfection in database management (Ph.D. Dissertation, University of Toronto), Toronto, Canada.

Vassiliou, Y. 1980. Functional dependencies and incomplete information. *Sixth International Conf. on Very Large Data Bases* 260-269.

Vassiliou, Y. 1979. Null values in database management: A denotational semantics approach. *ACM SIGMOD International Conf. on management of Data* 162-169.

Vlahos, O. 1967. *African Beginnings.* Greenwhich, Connecticut: Pawcett Publications, Inc.

Wang, K. and M. H. Graham. 1992. Constant-time maintainability: A generalization of independence. *ACM Trans. on Database Syst* 17, 2:201-246.

Wilkie, G. 1993. *Object-Oriented Software Engineering.* Reading, Massachusetts: Addison-Wesley Publishing Company.

Wilkinson, B. and M. Allen. 1999. *Parallel Programming: Techniques and Applications Using Networked Workstations and Parallel Computers.* Upper Saddle River, New Jersey: Prentice-Hall, Inc.

Williams, S. A. 1990. *Programming Models for Parallel Systems.* New York, New York: John Wiley and Sons, Inc.

Wikström, Åke. 1987. *Functional Programming Using Standard ML.* London, England: Prentice-Hall, Inc.

Wong, E. 1982. A statistical approach to incomplete information in database systems. *ACM Trans. on Database Syst.* 7, 3:470-488.

Wexler, J. 1989. *Concurrent Programming in Occam 2.* Chichester, England: Ellis Horwood Ltd.

Whiddett, D. 1987. *Concurrent Programming for Software Engineers.* Chichester, England: Ellis Horwood Ltd.

Winston, P. H. 1998. *On To Smalltalk.* Reading, Massachusetts: Addison-Wesley.

Yang, C.-C. 1986. *Relational Database*. Englewood Cliffs, New Jersey: Prentice-Hall.

Zaniolo, C., ed. 1987. Special issue on databases and logic. *Data Engineering* 10, 4. IEEE Computer Society.

Zaniolo, C. 1984. Database relations with null values. *Journal of Comp. and System Sc.* 28, 1:142-166.

Zaniolo, C. 1982. A new normal form for the design of relational database schemas. *ACM Trans. on Database Syst.* 7, 3:489-499.

Zaniolo, C. 1977. Relational views in a database system; support for queries. *IEEE Int. Conference on Computer Software and Applications* 267-275.

Zaniolo, C. 1976. Analysis and design of relational schemata for database systems (Ph.D. Dissertation, University of California Los Angeles), Los Angeles, California.

Zaniolo, C. and M. A. Melkanoff. 1981. On the design of relational database schemata. *ACM Trans. on database Syst.* 6, 1:1-47.

About the Author

Abdul Karim Bangura is Researcher-In-Residence at the Center for Global Peace and Assistant Professor of International Relations in the School of International Service at American University, and Director of The African Institution in Washington, DC. Bangura holds a Ph.D. in Political Science, a Ph.D. in Policy Sciences (concentration in Development Economics), a Ph.D. in Linguistics, a Ph.D. in Computer Science, and is working towards a fifth Ph.D. in Mathematics. He is the author of 19 books and more than 200 scholarly articles. He is the Editor-In-Chief of two refereed journals: the *Journal of Research Methodology and African Studies* and the *African Journal of Languages and Linguistics*. He is the President-Elect of the Association of Third World Studies, in addition to being a member of many and holding offices in several other scholarly organizations. He in the winner of many scholarly and community service awards. He also speaks about a dozen African and six European languages.